MEDITATIONS FOR INTERSPIRITUAL PRACTICE

The Spiritual Paths Series

Mandala: Creating an Authentic Spiritual Paths – An InterSpiritual Process by Edward W. Bastian

InterSpiritual Meditation: A Seven-Part Process from the World's Spiritual Traditions by Edward W. Bastian

Meditations for InterSpiritual Practice: A Collection of Practices from the World's Spiritual Traditions by Netanel Miles-Yépez

For more information on the Spiritual Paths Institute, its programs and Spiritual Paths seminars, and as well as courses in InterSpiritual Meditation, please visit: www. spiritualpaths.net / www.interspiritualmeditation.org.

MEDITATIONS FOR INTERSPIRITUAL PRACTICE

*A Collection of Practices from the
World's Spiritual Traditions*

Second Edition

Edited by
NETANEL MILES-YÉPEZ

Foreword by
EDWARD W. BASTIAN

The Spiritual Paths Series

Albion
Andalus
Boulder, Colorado
2015

"The old shall be renewed,
and the new shall be made holy."
— Rabbi Avraham Yitzhak Kook

Albion-Andalus Inc.
P. O. Box 19852
Boulder, CO 80308
www.albionandalus.com

Design and composition by Albion-Andalus Inc.
Cover design by Sari Wisenthal-Shore.
The "Flower of InterSpiritual Meditation" on the cover envisioned
by Edward W. Bastian and created by Lynda Rae.
Photo of Netanel Miles-Yépez by Don Senia Murray.

Manufactured in the United States of America

ISBN-13: 978-0692407592 (Albion-Andalus Books)
ISBN-10: 0692407596

For my uncle, Steven Paul Wallace,
of blessed memory

Contents

PART II
SELECTED READINGS
FROM THE WORLD'S SPIRITUAL TRADITIONS

ACKNOWLEDGMENTS

WITH GRATITUDE TO my friend and colleague, Edward W. Bastian, and to the many other wonderful contributors to this book: Swami Atmarupananda, Ozer Bergman, Tessa Bielecki, Ven. Bikkhu Bodhi, Ken Cohen, Father Dave Denny, Dr. John Allen Grimes, Camille Adams Helminski, Sheikh Kabir Helminski, Pir Zia Inayat-Khan, Don "Four Arrows" Jacobs, Yogi Nataraja Kallio, Dr. Michael Kearney, Father Thomas Keating, Sheikh Muhammad Jamal al-Jerrahi (Gregory Blann), Rabbi Jeff Roth, Rabbi Zalman Schachter-Shalomi, z"l, Grace Alvarez Sesma, Acharya Judith Simmer-Brown, and Dr. Alan Wallace. And I am especially grateful right now to my friends—Lasette Brown, Adam Bucko, Leigh Ann Dillinger, Eve Ilsen, Zvi Ish-Shalom, Rory McEntee, Deepa Patel, and Raj Seymour—and to the woman I love.

— N.M-Y.

FOREWORD

WITHIN EVERY RELIGION there is small population of dedicated contemplatives whose inner lives go mostly unnoticed by the general public. They might be monks, nuns, hermits, teachers, or regular folks living seemingly unremarkable lives. Their interior practices take them beneath the surface of religious rituals, prayers, songs, mantras, incantations and institutions. In their meditations, they relive the epiphanies of their founders and saints. Generation after generation, they safeguard and nurture the roots of profound spiritual practice. Without them, the heart of their tradition would simply stop beating.

For most of history, these individual contemplatives have not been exposed to the practices and principles of other traditions and the general public has been oblivious to the treasures in their midst. This is mostly because specialized training is required for each contemplative practice, and because the wisdom keepers have been separated from each other by oceans, mountains, deserts, religious boundaries and language. But now we live in an extraordinary time when lineage holders of the world's contemplative traditions can begin to share the hidden wisdom that has been transmitted from teacher to student over hundreds and even thousands of years. Today's population shifts and the Internet, along with new translations of esoteric texts, have enabled a sharing that was never possible before.

The Spiritual Paths Foundation is following in the footsteps of such InterSpiritual pathfinders as His Holiness the Dalai Lama, Father Thomas Merton, Father Thomas Keating and Rabbi Zalman Schachter-Shalomi. Through our classes and programs, we bring together contemplative lineage holders from many traditions to share the wisdom, methods, and experiences of their respective paths. In so doing, we ask them to speak *from* their own understanding and experience, rather than *for* their traditions. This is because the world's spiritual traditions are far too vast, too deep and diverse to be neatly summed-up in a single presentation or meditation.

InterSpirituality begins in silence. As Father Thomas Keating often says, "Silence is the first language of the divine." So when fellow contemplatives from many traditions come together, we are bathed and softened in the nectar of silence. Our individual spiritual identities are made permeable by the delicate mist of shared intention, experience and gentle speech. In our dialogue and teachings, we learn deeply from each other the fruits of contemplative wisdom and practice from our differing traditions. Just as travelers to foreign lands return to see more clearly their own homelands, our InterSpiritual journeys into other traditions help us to discern the refined nuances and gems of our own tradition as if for the first time. By traveling a while in other contemplative traditions, our own meditations become the vehicle for universal wisdom and kinship with people of all traditions. This is equally true for people without a tradition. For these practices awaken the divine potential dormant within their hearts and minds.

The result of this InterSpiritual process is that we never again see each other as 'the other.' The rigid boundaries of religious identity are dissolved as we clearly regard others as our self. There is a felt-sense of unity within our diversity, a unity that emerges from compassionate intention, shared experience, and a humility regarding our capacity for conceptual certainty of the ineffable. Our experience together is a celebration of the combined wisdom, creativity, and energy arising from our diversity.

This InterSpiritual experience is a foundation for global peace. It is the promised land wherein our human potential can be fulfilled; the safe harbor in which people of all religions can all find refuge; a universal covenant binding us to an integral, reciprocal and essential relationship with all of existence; a shared aesthetic in which we can walk hand-in-hand for the common good.

These pages contain the contemplative offerings of mature meditators from many traditions. In them, you will find both similarities and distinctions. You might gain insights to enrich your own practice or be inspired to engage in one more deeply than another. They have been carefully chosen and skillfully edited by Netanel Miles-Yépez who has been a close collaborator in the InterSpiritual work for many years. I am deeply grateful to him for compiling this volume and contributing to the emergence of InterSpiritual wisdom in our times.

Meditations for InterSpiritual Practice is a companion to my own book, *InterSpiritual Meditation,* in which I offer a simple contemplative liturgy which both experienced and aspiring meditators can practice on their own or together. In this process, each meditator engages in their own practice while at the same time contributing to a shared contemplative experience that is inclusive of the sum of its parts.

May these meditations enrich your personal practice and appreciation of the wisdom all the world's spiritual traditions. May they contribute to the peaceful co-existence, enlightenment, and flourishing of all beings.

DR. EDWARD W. BASTIAN
Santa Barbara Harbor, California, 2015

INTRODUCTION

MEDITATIONS FOR INTERSPIRITUAL PRACTICE is not a title I can expect to speak for itself today. It is hard enough to describe meditation to most people in an accurate way without throwing a phrase like 'InterSpiritual practice' into the mix. Nevertheless, I felt it was necessary to use this title for two reasons. First, although this book can certainly stand alone, it is also a companion to Edward Bastian's *InterSpiritual Meditation,* thus necessitating some similarity in titles.[1] But beyond that practical necessity is a more current and spiritually oriented need to make a statement about InterSpirituality.

For many of us involved in deeply meaningful dialogues with persons of other spiritual traditions today, the conventional terms 'inter-faith,' 'inter-religious,' and 'pluralism,' no longer serve to describe what it is we are doing. Pluralism's emphasis on 'tolerance,' while positive in itself, barely scratches the surface of this dialogue. And while 'inter-faith' and 'inter-religious' go much further in this regard, they are nevertheless limited by the boundaries of faith and religion. That is to say, the encounter does not take place between 'religions' or 'representatives of religions,' but between individual human beings who happen to have different religious commitments. Nor is religion necessarily the currency exchanged; religious ideas and information about one another's religion are *not* the focus of the dialogue. The focus is more often the deep structures shared by different spiritual traditions, spiritual experience, and the techniques used to achieve it.

---

1 Edward W. Bastian, *InterSpiritual Meditation: A Seven-Step Process drawn from the World's Spiritual Traditions,* Boulder, CO: Albion-Andalus Books, 2015.

It is for this reason that Christian innovators like Brother Wayne Teasdale and Father Matthew Fox began to talk about "interspirituality" and "deep ecumenism."[22] In both, the dialogue is seen as an opportunity to learn about *oneself* while in full engagement with another, opening oneself to change. For in any true listening, there is always the possibility of being changed by the encounter. One might even choose to participate in the practices of another religious tradition, to engage in experiential learning or "participatory epistemology" as Rabbi Zalman Schachter-Shalomi, one of this volume's contributors, likes to say. Such knowledge, he suggests, can open one up to an understanding of the "basic technology" beneath the religious exterior, allowing us to discern what is essential from what is accidental (in the philosophical sense) in our own religious traditions. In many ways, this is what the early Indologist Max Müller had in mind when he paraphrased Goethe, saying, "He who knows only one religion, knows none."

From this perspective, InterSpiritual dialogue might be seen as a kind of diagnostic to be run on our own spiritual lives and our religious traditions—to see how well each is functioning—and to be used as a tool for refining our own understanding of scripture and spiritual experience.

INTERSPIRITUAL MEDITATION

In the late 1990's, Edward Bastian, a member of the famous Snowmass Interreligious Conference (which met privately for annual retreats from 1984 to the present), began to dream of a meditation practice that could be shared by people of different religious traditions.[33] This dream was inspired by the InterSpiritually oriented dialogue of the Snowmass Conference itself which punctuated its dialogues with periods of silent group meditation. For Bastian, a long-time Buddhist meditator, these periods of meditation were actually the highlight of the retreat and seemed to bring all of the disparate elements of the dialogue

---

2 See Wayne Teasdale, *The Mystic Heart: Discovering a Universal Spirituality in the World's Religions,* Novato, California: New World Library, 1999 and Matthew Fox, *One River, Many Wells: Wisdom Springing from Global Faiths,* New York: Jeremy P. Tarcher/Putnam, 2000.
3 See Netanel Miles-Yépez, ed., *The Common Heart: An Experience of Interreligious Dialogue,* New York: Lantern Books, 2006.

together. Nevertheless, he felt the meditation had no focus. It was simply a period in which the teachers of different traditions could sit down in silence together and pursue their separate meditation and prayer practices. Thus, he wondered if they might not refine the process and make it more purposeful. Over the next ten years, he began his own dialogue with teachers of other traditions, hoping to discern the common elements of meditative practice and to distill these elements into a unique InterSpiritual practice, allowing people of different traditions to meditate together, sharing one process, while still keeping what is unique to their own traditions intact.

Thus, his book, *InterSpiritual Meditation* offers a seven-part process that can be practiced alone, in the company of people from the same tradition, or with people from many different traditions. It is designed to bring about a shared experience of the sacred which may bring a little more harmony into our divided world. It is called 'InterSpiritual Meditation' because it draws together the key components of meditative processes found in many of the world's religions to create an 'InterSpiritual Consciousness.' It is not meant to replace a person's spiritual practice, but is simply a process through which like-minded individuals can begin to harmonize the unique contributions of each spiritual tradition, embracing the marvelous spiritual diversity that has been given us.

MEDITATIONS FOR INTERSPIRITUAL PRACTICE

The purpose of this particular volume is to provide the InterSpiritually inclined meditator with resources for further exploration. Whether they would like to take a second look at the practices of their own tradition, explore the practices of another tradition, or compare practices and find what suits them best, I believe this book will be of use.

As a companion to Edward Bastian's *InterSpiritual Meditation,* it has another more specific purpose. Because the InterSpiritual Meditation process does not impose a specific meditation technique, but rather recommends the use of an appropriate technique of your own choosing, I felt it was necessary to gather a useful selection of meditative and contemplative practices from different traditions from which to choose. As all seven steps in the process allow for the possibility of introducing a meditation or prayer practice of some kind, I have chosen to include at least three practices from each of the world's major religious traditions.[44] Moreover, I have also included verses from these same traditions on seven meditation themes that parallel the seven steps of the InterSpiritual Meditation process. Most of these are taken from the scriptures of the world's traditions, though some come from oral sources, and a few from later traditions.

Though some people may consider it a stretch to call all of the practices suggested in this book, 'meditations,' it was done for the sake of inclusivity, to broaden the narrow notion of meditation many people have today, and to deepen our understanding. The broader definition which Edward Bastian and I have agreed upon for the purposes of our own dialogue, and for use in these two volumes is this:

> Meditation is a technique for attuning consciousness, which—depending on the individual, the technique used, and the spiritual context in which it is done—may lead to altered states of awareness (including, profound focus and tranquility), usually considered beneficial or transformative for individuals and groups.

Thus, we have prayer practices, discursive meditations or contemplations, and non-discursive, centering practices, all in the same book, and all considered meditations of one variety or another. In this way, we hope to give the user a wide range of resources and good idea of the way similar practices are uniquely nuanced in different spiritual traditions.

BUDDHISM

Though the Buddhist practices in this volume would appear to come primarily from Tibetan Buddhism, the reader will soon find that the Theravadin Buddhist tradition of Southeast Asia is also represented here in a significant way, ultimately giving one a sense of just how much is actually shared by these culturally disparate traditions.

---

4 Step 5 of the Inter-Spiritual Meditation process recommends a technique for cultivating mindfulness, and Step 6 a specific contemplation; however, all of the steps may be adapted for use with a specific meditation.

In "Cultivating Tranquil Focus & Transcendental Insight," Edward Bastian a longtime student of the Gelugpa school of Tibetan Buddhism, introduces us to Buddhism's most foundational meditative practice called *Shamatha-Vipashyana,* Sanskrit for 'tranquil focus' and 'transcendental insight.' In this practice, the Buddhist meditator learns to quell the mind's incessant activity, paving the way for a truly mindful awareness of our thoughts, feelings and sensations, to which we may then apply "analytical wisdom."

This article is followed by "The Four Applications of Mindfulness," in which Alan Wallace (also thoroughly trained in the Gelugpa school of Tibetan Buddhism) uses his broad knowledge of philosophy and science to describe the analytical meditation for which *Shamatha* provides the ground; i.e., "careful observation and consideration of the body, feelings, mental states, and mental objects of oneself and of others."

Though both Alan Wallace and Edward Bastian were trained in the Tibetan Buddhist tradition, which usually relies on later Mahayana presentations of Buddhist teachings in Sanskrit and upon Tibetan commentaries, it is interesting to note that both have based their presentations in this book on the teachings of the great Pali text of the early Theravadin Buddhist tradition called the *Mahasatipatthanasutta.* In so doing, they have closed the gap between these two noble traditions and demonstrated how much is really shared by the various Buddhist lineages in different cultures.

Finally, Judith Simmer-Brown, a Tibetan Buddhist *acharya* (senior teacher) of the Karma-Kagyu lineage of Chogyam Trungpa Rinpoche, introduces us to a Buddhist contemplative practice for cultivating compassion called *tonglen* in "The Practice of Giving & Receiving." In this practice, one uses the inhalation and exhalation pattern of *Shamatha* meditation to unselfishly take-in "those things we would rather avoid," and to intentionally "share what we would rather keep for ourselves."

CHRISTIANITY

The Christian practices in the book come from the Catholic tradition, though they are in no way intended to be for Catholics alone. It is simply that the contemplative orders of Catholicism specialized in such practices for centuries and have thus become the primary merchants of this precious commodity in our time.

In "Finding Intimacy with God," Father Thomas Keating, a Cistercian monk and one of the great contemplative teachers of our time, gives us a simple, elegant introduction to Centering Prayer, a meditative practice based on indications in the Christian spiritual classic, *The Cloud of Unknowing.*

This practice was revived in the mid-1970s by Father William Meninger, the former retreat master at St. Joseph's Abbey which Father Thomas served as abbot until 1981. Later, Father Thomas, Father William, and their fellow monk, Father Basil Pennington began to teach Centering Prayer all over the world, in time creating a major contemplative movement. Today, the movement is directed by Contemplative Outreach, which Father Thomas founded in 1984.

The final two Christian practices come from two well-known Carmelite hermits in southern Colorado, Father David Denny and Tessa Bielecki, formerly mother abbess of the Spiritual Life Institute. In "Making the Soul Fertile," Father Dave introduces us to the Christian tradition of *meditatio,* discursive meditation, or disciplined contemplation of a particular spiritual theme. Quoting a 12th century Christian monastic, he tells us: "Meditation is the busy application of the mind to seek with the help of one's own reason for knowledge of hidden truth."

Then Tessa Bielecki gives us a new perspective on the ancient Christian prayer known as The Angelus, recited three times a day by the faithful. In her article, "The Angelus—A Mindfulness Practice," Bielecki explores the inner dimensions of the practice, its words, and how it might be used in our daily lives: "How is the Angelus a valuable mindfulness practice?" she asks. "When the bells begin to ring, you completely stop whatever you're doing and attend to the prayer."

HINDUISM

The Hindu practices in this book represent only a tiny fraction of the vast array of approaches to spiritual realization in the Hindu tradition. Nevertheless, they are among the most efficacious and useful for practitioners today.

The first article, "The Breath Within the Breath" by Yogi Nataraja

Kallio, a teacher of Yoga and Yoga philosophy, introduces us to the Yogic breath practice called *pranayama,* which is considered an essential tool for "creating health and harmony in the body, but also for the expansion of consciousness and the realization of our true nature." While Yoga *asana* or posture practice is mainstream today, many of the deeper elements of *pranayama* and Yogic meditation are not. Therefore, this article may be looked to as an essential introduction to breath practice for modern Yoga practitioners.

This is followed by an entirely different type of meditation, "The Practice of Self-Enquiry" by the Advaitin philosopher, John Allen Grimes. This analytical meditation practice of the non-dualist Advaita Vedanta school of philosophy, according to Grimes, "is a gentle technique that bypasses the usual repressive methods of controlling the mind. It is not an exercise in concentration or meditation, nor does it aim at suppressing thoughts. It merely invokes awareness of the source from which the mind, and thus all meditation techniques, spring." Through this enquiry, we transcend the notion of the limited self and come to realize our identity of with the true Self of all Being, *Brahman.*

Finally, in "The Infinite Word," Swami Atmarupananda, a senior monk of the Ramakrishna Order, helps us to explore the origins, inner dimensions and practice of *mantra japa,* the meditational use of sacred words and phrases in rhythmic repetition, aloud or mentally. A *mantra,* he tells us, is "a tool of transcendence," the Infinite Word which is "indeed the supreme *Brahman.*"

INDIGENOUS SPIRITUALITY

This was the most difficult group of articles to assemble for a variety of reasons, but all the more precious for the trouble. The practices of indigenous traditions are often left out of such collections—sometimes because the editor doesn't wish to be accused of cultural appropriation, sometimes because authentic teachers of these traditions are hard to find or will not speak on these subjects, and sometimes because the practices do not appear to fit within the more conventional categories of religious practice. Fortunately, I was led to the doorstep of three authentic practitioners of indigenous wisdom who were generous enough to explain their beliefs and practices in a way that satisfies both the reader and the integrity of their traditions. Though some of these practices are less amenable to use with the InterSpiritual Meditation process than others, they are nonetheless valuable as resources for those who belong to these traditions, and in helping us to understand their place in the wider context of the world's meditation traditions.

The first of these articles, "Entering the Flower World: A Mexican Path to the Soul" by *curandera* (healer) Grace Alvarez Sesma, introduces us to an authentic Sunrise-Sunset meditation and gives us a glimpse into the wonderfully rich world of traditional Mexican (Aztec and Maya) religious belief preserved in the syncretic healing tradition called *Curanderismo*.

Then, Don "Four Arrows" Jacobs, in a two-part article called "The Inipi Ceremony & Crying for a Vision," explores the issues of cultural appropriation while attempting to explain the significance of the Lakota purification ceremony and vision quest he learned during his years as a Sun Dancer with the Oglala on the Pine Ridge Indian Reservation.

Finally, in "Returning to Sacred Ground," Michael Kearney, an Irish-born specialist in the psycho-spiritual aspects of end-of-life care, acquaints us with the re-emerging tradition of indigenous Celtic spirituality and its own nature-based meditation.

ISLAM

The four articles on Islamic meditation in this volume come from teachers of the Sufi mystical tradition and highlight both the rich spiritual heritage of Islam and the sophistication of its esoteric practices.

In "The Elemental Purification Breaths," Pir Zia Inayat-Khan, the grandson of the great Indian Sufi master Hazrat Inayat Khan and president of the Sufi Order International, not only introduces us to a foundational breathing practice of the Chishti-Inayati Sufis, but also shows us the origins of Sufism in Islam and how the Chishti tradition of Sufism evolved meditation practices through the centuries and came to a unique fusion of Indic and Islamic practice.

Sheikh Muhammad Jamal al-Jerrahi's "The Examination of Conscience" guides us through the Muslim Sufi contemplative practice known as *muhasaba*, "a time-honored spiritual practice used to account for one's daily behavior and to scrutinize one's hidden motivations and tendencies as they manifest in everyday life."

After this, Sheikh Kabir Helminski of the Mevlevi Order founded by the poet Rumi, in "The Path of Radical Remembrance," introduces us to the central practice of Sufism, *zikr* or 'remembrance.' Using a combination of traditional sources and his own unique perspective, Sheikh Kabir shows how the practice of *zikr* transfers remembrance of God "from the tongue to the mind, from the mind to the feelings and the deeper levels of the personality, until its reality is established in the core of the human being."

Finally, Sheikha Camille Helminski, Sheikh Kabir's wife and teaching partner, gives us "The Prayer of Light" once recited each morning by Rumi, and now recited daily by all Mevlevi Sufis. This is a practice she recommends including in one's daily practice after prayer or silent meditation.

JUDAISM

In the last thirty years, the largely hidden traditions of Jewish meditation have begun to reemerge and take center stage in many parts of the Jewish world. Some of these were buried in medieval texts, while others were for a long time thought to be the exclusive property of particular Hasidic mystical sects. Much of the credit for bringing these traditions to light goes to Rabbi Zalman Schachter-Shalomi and Rabbi Aryeh Kaplan, two profoundly learned teachers of Jewish mysticism who both understood that it was finally time to reveal these practices. But credit must also be given to the Habad and Breslov lineages of Hasidim for reaching out to the modern world and seeking to make their own meditation traditions available to Jews everywhere.

In the first article, "Breathing the Divine Name," Rabbi Jeff Roth, a longtime student of Jewish meditation and spiritual practice, teaches us a medieval breathing technique found in the mystical writings of the early kabbalist, Rabbi Yosef ibn Gikatilla, showing us how "God's name is connected to the breath."

Then, the late Rabbi Zalman Schachter-Shalomi, the *doyen* of Jewish meditation himself, introduces us to the contemplative practice known as *hitbonenut* in "The Practice of Self-Understanding." This practice, which comes from the Habad Hasidic tradition in which Schachter-Shalomi was trained, is "a special technique of discursive meditation or contemplation, during which one thoroughly explores a spiritual concept, filling one's consciousness with it and thus brings about change in one's life."

Finally, Ozer Bergman, a prominent teacher of Breslov Hasidism, in "Pouring Out Your Heart to God," helps us to understand the powerful practice of the Hasidic master, Rebbe Nahman of Breslov called *hitbodedut,* in which you "pour out your heart to God as you would to a true, good friend."

TAOISM

In seeking Taoist teachers to talk about Taoist meditation, I encountered more difficulty than I would have imagined. There were simply fewer authentic teachers of Taoism writing in English than I expected; and among those who were, many were not actually masters of the tradition, while others considered themselves merely translators and not teachers.

Fortunately, I was able to find both in Kenneth Cohen, a well-known Qigong Master and Taoist scholar. Because I was not able to identify other teachers of the tradition in time for the publication of this book, he offered to write an article ("The Breath of Tao") that would at once introduce us to Taoism, contextualize the tradition of Taoist meditation, and give us "two of the most classic and revered Taoist meditations," in which we "learn to breathe innocently and deeply like a newborn baby," for "breathing teaches us to surrender to the wisdom of the Tao as manifest in our body's natural rhythms."

In this humble collection of meditations, I sincerely hope you will find something useful for your own practice, whether it is a practice that will help to transform your life, a deeper understanding of your existing meditative practice, or just a better appreciation of the marvelous diversity of meditation practices in the world's spiritual traditions. I pray that the wisdom you may gain from it will be of benefit in your life, and of benefit to our world.

NETANEL MILES-YÉPEZ
Boulder, Colorado 2015

PART I
SELECTED PRACTICES FROM
THE WORLD'S SPIRITUAL TRADITIONS

Buddhist Practices

CULTIVATING TRANQUIL FOCUS & TRANSCENDENTAL INSIGHT

Edward W. Bastian

THE LIFE STORY of the Buddha has resonance for all of us who are compelled to discover the truth of our existence and the path to eternal happiness. For here was a human being endowed with every possible material and sensual pleasure, and yet, these could not satisfy his longing. So he set off on a lonely and difficult journey to discover the truth of all existence and the source of happiness. And throughout history, countless people have been inspired to do the same by the Buddha's heroic example.

The Buddha studied with the great teachers of his time and experienced the fruit of their practices: he experimented with extreme austerity; he begged for food; he absorbed the major metaphysical teachings of India, meditating on the possible unity of his individual soul *(atman)* with the ultimate universal creator *(Brahman);* and he nearly died of starvation for fear of harming other living beings. Finally, he decided to simply sit beneath a tree until the truth emerged. After forty-nine days and nights of meditating he experienced the omniscience of enlightenment, liberation from the causes of suffering and the bliss of *Nirvana*. For the next forty-five years, he taught others to experience this for themselves and laid the foundation for one of the world's great spiritual traditions.

Based on his own experience, he concluded that everyone had the potential to see the true nature of existence, to achieve eternal enlightenment and bliss, and to help others achieve the same goals. But doing this would require a skillful combination of wisdom and compassionate service.

The Buddha found that the cause of our suffering is our attachment to the notion of an independent, unchanging soul, and the idea that the objects we perceive exist independently, causing us to see them as other than they are. We mistakenly believe that these objects are intrinsically desirable or undesirable, and therefore, have the power to make us happy or sad. To heal us of this misperception, the Buddha taught us that that things and people are impermanent, interdependent, and empty of intrinsic existence.

It is only our own ignorance, desire and attachment that causes things to be desirable and undesirable, beautiful and ugly. People and things don't cause us to see them as good or bad. Rather, we impose that judgment on them. We project our ignorance and emotions on them and this causes us to be in a state of anxiety, emotional unrest and suffering.

How do we stop this incessant projection? How do we stop clinging to our judgments about people and things? How do we come to grips with the fact that the external word is not what it seems to be? How do we recondition our mind to see things as they are and to behave compassionately towards others?

For the Buddha, the answer is meditation.

In the *Satipatthanasutta,* which contains some of his earliest teachings, it says:

> [T]his is the direct path for the purification of beings, for the surmounting of sorrow and lamentation, for the disappearance of suffering *(dukkha)* and discontent, for acquiring the true method, for the realizations of Nirvana *(Nibbana),* namely, the four true foundations *(satipatthanas).*
>
> What are the four? Here, [...] in regard to the body (feelings, mind, phenomena) a [meditator] abides contemplating the body, diligent, clearly knowing, and mindful, free from desires and discontent in regard to the world.

Here, the Buddha is teaching us to focus our attention solely on our body, feelings, mind and all existents. This tranquil, undistracted focus is called *shamatha,* and it is the first step toward Mindfulness. *Shamatha* training begins by cultivating a calm, single-pointed focus on the constituents of our being and the objects of our perception.

Shamatha generally begins with undistracted attention to

breathing. Then, once our mind is calm and undistracted, we can shift our attention to other aspects of the body like our posture, movements, anatomical parts, elements, and even our future corpse in decay. Once we have completed a *shamatha*-scan of our body, we focus on our feelings, our mind, and everything that we perceive *(dhammas)*. *Shamatha* can be practiced while sitting, standing, walking or lying down. It enables us to be exquisitely aware of all aspects of our being and to attune our words, thoughts, and actions to our compassionate intention for living. It is the foundational practice of many Buddhist meditations.

Shamatha, or Mindfulness meditation, can have wondrous effects on the body and mind. It can quell stress, anxiety, hypertension, high blood pressure, and help cure the myriad diseases that stem from these. It is also said to give way to a range of psychic abilities, including clairvoyance. But it is just the first step along the Buddhist path of meditation. For as the 8th-century Buddhist teacher Kamalashila said in his "Stages of Meditation":

> Yogis cannot eliminate mental obscurations merely by familiarizing themselves with calm abiding meditation alone. It will only suppress the disturbing emotions and delusions temporarily. Without the light of wisdom, the latent potential of the disturbing emotions cannot be thoroughly destroyed, and therefore, their complete destruction will not be possible.

Knowing this, the Buddha provided us with further instructions in the *Satipatthanasutta:*

> He abides contemplating the nature of both the arising and passing away in the body (feelings, mind, phenomena). Mindfulness that 'there is a body' is established in him to the extent necessary for bare knowledge and continuous mindfulness. And he abides independent, not clinging to anything in the world.

Here, the Buddha instructs us on the second phase of meditation called *vipashyana,* often translated as 'transcendental insight.' At this stage in the meditation, having employed *shamatha* to focus on an object (or a category meditational objects), the meditator applies analytical wisdom to that object. This is the wisdom that knows all phenomena to be constantly "rising and passing away."

It knows that all phenomena are interdependent and conditioned by the projections of the mind that perceives them. Or, as the Buddhist philosopher Nagarjuna stated it in his "Seventy Verses on Emptiness":

> All things arise from causes and conditions;
> To view them as real is ignorance;
> From this arises the twelve interdependent links.

One of the Buddha's unique contributions to our global spiritual heritage is his proposition that liberation gradually emerges by eliminating the causes of our bondage. Truth and freedom naturally arise once we eliminate the ignorance, attachment and desire that cloud our minds. Having removed the clouds, we are able to perceive the true nature of reality. Based on this wisdom we are truly able to serve others.

The combination of *shamatha* and *vipashyana* are designed to eliminate the obstacles to our enlightenment. The following passage from the "Heart Sutra" takes this a step further. Here, in addition to seeing just the "rising and falling away" of all phenomena, we are instructed to see that all things are also "empty of intrinsic existence":

> Shariputra, a noble son or noble daughter who so wishes to engage in the practice of the profound perfection of wisdom should clearly see this way: They should see perfectly that even the five aggregates are empty of intrinsic existence. Form is emptiness, emptiness is form. Emptiness is not other than form, form too is not other than emptiness. Likewise, feelings, perceptions, mental formations, and consciousness are all empty.

Here we are taught to hold each of the five aggregates (form, feelings, perceptions, mental formations and consciousness) as the objects of *shamatha* meditation, and then through *vipashyana* meditation, to directly perceive the fact that they are empty of intrinsic existence. 'Emptiness of intrinsic of existence' is a negative way or saying that all phenomena are impermanent and interdependent. That is, things are 'empty' of the capacity of existing permanently, intrinsically and independently. The meditative laser-beam of emptiness dissolves our ignorance, desire, and attachment, thus freeing our minds to see things as they *really* are.

So we see that *shamatha* and *vipashyana* remain the consistent meditative thread through many types of Buddhist meditation. This combination of tranquil focus and transcendental insight is meant to help us experience the very same realization as the Buddha had, to shed clinging and attachment to projected illusions, and to experience the bliss and liberation that comes when our mind is purified.

As the great master Shantideva says in Chapter 8 of his "Way of the Bodhisattva":

> Cultivating diligence as just described,
> In concentration I will place my mind.
> For those whose minds are slack and wandering
> Are caught between the fangs of the afflictions.
>
> In solitude, the mind and body
> Are not troubled by distraction.
> Therefore, leave this worldly life
> And totally abandon mental wandering.
>
> Because of loved ones and desire for gain,
> We fail to turn away from worldly things.
> These, then, are the first things to renounce.
> The prudent should conduct themselves like this.
>
> Penetrative insight joined with calm abiding
> Utterly eradicates afflicted states.
> Knowing this, first search for calm abiding,
> Found by people who are happy to be free from worldly ties.

SHAMATHA AND VIPASHYANA:
A SAMPLE MEDITATION SESSION

We assume a relaxed, meditative posture in a quiet spot where distractions and interruptions are minimal.

Then, we set our intention thus: may this meditation generate wisdom to help others to be enlightened and free from suffering.

We begin our *shamatha* meditation by focusing our attention on the breath. For the next few minutes, we concentrate solely on the feeling of the air caressing the entrance of our nostrils.

We allow our whole body to relax and feel the tranquility of one-pointed attention on our breathing. We gently breathe-in for six seconds, hold our breath for four seconds, and exhale for six seconds. We find our own natural rhythm for breathing.

We imagine our conscious awareness riding on this smooth, subtle stream of air as it travels through our nasal passages, down the back of our throat, into our lungs, and expanding out to the extremities of our chest. We feel the oxygen flowing to every living cell in our body.

Simultaneously, from the background of our mind, we watch for any distracting sounds, sensations, thoughts, memories or daydreams. We let our "mental spy" keep a look out from the background of our consciousness. When it spots an incoming distraction, we simply name it—a sound, an image, a memory, a sensation—and let it dissolve like a cloud dissipating into the blue sky.

This calm focus on breathing is the beginning stage of *shamatha* meditation. For the next few minutes, we keep our attention solely on the breath as it enters and circulates throughout our entire system.

Next, we engage the *vipashyana* phase of our meditation. Keeping tranquil focus, we observe how our breath rises and falls away. We observe the impermanence and the interdependence of breathing. For example, we observe how breathing-in the oxygen from the earth's plants nourishes the trillions of living the cells of our body. We observe how our out-breath of carbon dioxide nourishes these plants in turn. We become fully absorbed in the interdependent reciprocity of being.

Finally, we observe how our breath is empty, our bodily cells are empty, how all phenomena are empty of permanence and intrinsic existence. We become fully absorbed in this insight about the emptiness of all phenomena.

In this way, the insight of our *vipashyana* meditation

rests on the tranquil focus of our *shamatha* meditation. They become two essential components a single meditative session. Gradually, we apply these to our body, feelings, mind, and all phenomena that appear in our consciousness. In so doing, our calm and compassionate wisdom flourishes along with the profound fulfillment of serving others.

DR. EDWARD W. BASTIAN earned a Ph.D. in Buddhist studies and Western philosophy from the University of Wisconsin, conducting research for a number of years in India as a Fulbright Fellow. In India, he lived in Tibetan monasteries and studied Indian philosophy and religion at Banares Hindu University. He later taught courses and moderated discussions on religion for the Smithsonian Institution.

Bastian is also the executive producer for a series of six award-winning television programs on religion in India, Bhutan, and Japan for the BBC, and produced a series of three films on Tibetan Buddhism. Presently, he is president of Spiritual Paths Foundation, which produces seminars, books, television programs, and a Web site on spirituality, based on a methodology he has developed in collaboration with authentic exemplars from the world's major spiritual traditions. He is the author of *InterSpiritual Meditation: A Seven-Step Process from the World's Spiritual Traditions*, and co-author of the award-winning book, *Living Fully, Dying Well: Reflecting on Death to Find Your Life's Meaning*.

THE FOUR APPLICATIONS OF MINDFULNESS

Dr. B. Alan Wallace

THE CULTIVATION OF COMPASSION is like a silken thread that runs through and connects all the pearls of Buddhist meditative practices. Compassion is based upon empathy, but in a very deep sense insight into the nature of oneself, others, and the relation between oneself and the rest of the world is also based upon empathy. Moreover, a common Buddhist adage states the compassion without wisdom is bondage, and wisdom without compassion is just another form of bondage. Thus, wisdom and compassion must be cultivated together and empathy is a common root of both.

The classic Buddhist matrix of meditative practices known as the four applications of mindfulness is based on the *Satipatthanasutta*, the most revered of all Buddhist discourses in the Theravada Buddhist tradition.[1] This practice entails the careful observation and consideration of the body, feelings, mental states, and mental objects of oneself and of others. A common theme to each of these four applications of mindfulness is first considering these elements of one's own being, then attending to these same phenomena in others, and finally shifting one's attention back and forth between self and others. Especially in this final phase of practice, one engages in what has recently been called *reiterated empathy*, in which one imaginatively views one's own psycho-physical processes from a 'second-person' perspective. That is, I view my body and mind from what I imagine to be your perspective, so that I begin to sense my own presence not only 'from within' but 'from without.' Such practice leads to the insight that the second-person

1 For a translation of this discourse, together with a modern commentary see Nyanaponika Thera, *The Heart of Buddhist Meditation,* New York: Samuel Weiser, 1973.

perspective on one's own being is just as 'real' as the first-person perspective; and neither exists independently of the other.

Another of the central aims of these four applications of mindfulness is to distinguish between the phenomena that are presented to our six modes of perception and the conceptual superimpositions that we often unconsciously and involuntarily impute upon those phenomena, including labels, categories, and thoughts aroused by our emotional reactions. The Buddha summed up this theme when he declared, "In what is seen there should be only the seen; in what is heard, only the heard; in what is sensed, only the sensed; in what is perceived mentally, only the mentally perceived."[2]

The first subject for the close application of mindfulness is the body, for this is our physical basis in reality, on which we most readily identify our own whereabouts and distinguish ourselves from others. The Buddha quintessentially describes this practice as follows:

> One dwells observing the body as the body internally, or one dwells observing the body as the body externally, or one dwells observing the body as the body both internally and externally.[3]

In Pali (the language in which the Buddha's teachings were first recorded) the term translated here as 'observing' (*anupassati*) has the various meanings of observe, contemplate and consider, which override any strict demarcation between pure perception versus conceptual reflection. It means taking in the observed phenomena as fully as possible, both perceptually and conceptually, while still being sensitive to practical distinctions between what is presented to the senses and what is superimposed upon them. Such practice is done not only while sitting quietly in meditation, but while engaging in the various postures of walking, standing, sitting and lying down, as well as the activities of looking, bending, stretching, dressing, eating, drinking, excreting, speaking, keeping silent, staying awake and falling asleep.[4]

---

2 *Udana* 1:10.
3 *Satipatthanasutta* 5.
4 For a discussion of observing the four subjects of mindfulness inwardly, outwardly, and both inwardly and outwardly see Nyanaponika Thera, *The Heart of Buddhist Meditation*, New York: Samuel Weiser, 1973.

As one first attends to one's own body, one observes, among other things, the various events or factors that give rise to the emergence and dissolution of one's own experiences of and in the body. By *observing* one's own body, rather than simply *identifying* with it, one cultivates a kind of self-alterity, by experiencing one's own body simply as a matrix of phenomena, rather than as a self. Then, on the basis of the experiential insights gained in this way, one perceptually observes the body of another, experiencing that also as a matrix of phenomena. Finally, one alternates between observing both one's own and another's body, perceiving qualities that are unique to each one, as well as discerning common characteristics, which might include events that lead to the emergence and dissolution of body-events from moment to moment.

The most important common characteristic between one's own and others' bodies is that none of them either is or contains a self or personal identity. They are simply phenomena arising in dependence upon prior causes and conditions. In this way, one begins to break down the reified sense of the locality of one's own presence as being solely within the confines of one's own body. As William James reminds us, phenomenologically speaking, *"For the moment, what we attend to is reality . . ."*[5] By habitually failing to attend either to one's own body or those of others, the bodies that we disregard are eventually not counted as an existents at all. As James comments, "they are not even treated as appearances; they are treated as if they were mere waste, equivalent to nothing at all."[6] Moreover, by attending internally, externally, and finally internally and externally in immediate succession, one balances out any biases of attention one may have as a result of one's own introverted or extraverted disposition. In addition, in this final phase of alternating the attention between self and others, one is in a position to observe relationships between self and others that may not be apparent as long as one is focused on one to the exclusion of others. And as James cogently argues, very much in accordance with Buddhist principles, *"the relations that connect experiences must themselves be experienced relations, and any kind of relation experienced must be accounted a 'real' as anything else in the system."*[7]

5 William James, *The Principles of Psychology,* 322.
6 Ibid., 290-91.
7 William James, ed. John J. McDermott, *The Writings of William James: A Comprehensive Edition,* 195.

In the traditional practice of applying mindfulness to feelings, one observes the arising and dissolution of the three basic kinds of feelings of physical and mental pleasure, pain, and indifference in oneself, others, and alternately between oneself and others. Other more complex affective states are left to the next practice, but special attention is given to pleasant and unpleasant feelings because these have such an enormous effect on the kinds of choices we make, and the ways we conduct ourselves. According to Buddhism, for all sentient beings the most fundamental drive is to experience pleasure and joy and to avoid pain and suffering. Buddhist literature far more often makes references to "all sentient beings" who share this common desire than it does to "all human beings" alone. This is an indication that Buddhism is rightly characterized as more biocentric than anthropocentric.

While classical cognitive science has been 'cognocentric,' in the sense of maintaining that humans are cognizers first and foremost, recent advances in affective neuroscience suggest that emotions are primary and cognition has a secondary role as its organizing influence. According to Buddhism, neither cognition nor emotion is primary; rather, they are co-emergent, neither one capable of existing without the other. It is important to bear in mind, however, that the feeling of indifference, which some might regard as being an *absence* of feeling, is regarded in Buddhism as also being an affective state.

When observing the arising, presence and dissolution of feelings firsthand, one recognizes that they are not experienced by any means solely in the head, but rather in various regions throughout the body. And some do not appear to have any identifiable location at all. When it comes to empathetically attending to others' joys and sorrows, pleasures and pains, one can legitimately ask: are such 'observations' of others' internal affective states strictly inferential? That is, are these observations really conceptual conclusions based upon perceived outward signs of affective states? Or might this type of empathetic awareness be more direct, more akin to perception? I am not aware that either Buddhism or modern science has reached a consensus regarding these questions, but I believe they are worthy of careful consideration.

In the cultivation of mindfulness of mental states, one follows the threefold sequence as above, while observing the mind as it is affected by different affective and cognitive states such as craving, hatred, delusion, anxiety, elation, concentration and agitation. The aim of this practice is explicitly therapeutic in nature. Some affective and cognitive states are conducive to one's own and other's well-being while others are harmful. By attending closely to the factors that give rise to a wide range of mental processes, and by observing the effects they have on oneself and others, one begins to recognize through experience those processes that are conducive to one's own and others' well-being and those that are destructive. In this way, one identifies the distinctions between wholesome and unwholesome mental states. In particular, like a physician diagnosing an illness, one pays special attention to what Buddhism calls "mental afflictions," which can be identified by the criterion that they disrupt the balance and equilibrium of the mind. While some wholesome mental processes such as compassion may indeed disturb the calm of the mind, this disruption is not deep and its long-term effects on one's mental states and behavior are healthy. Other mental processes, however, such as resentment, have a deep and harmful impact on one's cognitive and affective health, as well as one's subsequent behavior, so they are deemed mental afflictions.

As in the previous practices of attending mindfully to the body and feelings, in this phase of the practice one observes one's own and others' mental processes simply as impersonal phenomena, arising in dependence upon prior causes and conditions. In particular, one pays special attention to the duration of these mental states: how long does each one last, and for as long as it lasts does it exist as a stable entity persisting through time or as a sequence of momentary events? When one observes a process in one's own mental continuum, is it affected by the sheer fact of being observed? Is it possible to observe one mental state with an awareness that is not itself in that same state? For example, is it possible to observe anger with an un-angry mind? Does one observe an intentional mental process *while* it is occurring, or is such mindfulness always retrospective? It is important to bear in mind that the Pali term commonly translated as 'mindfulness' (*sati*) also has the connotation of 'recollection,' implying that many, if not all acts of mindfulness may actually be modes of short-term recall. The issue of observer-participancy is obviously crucial to the first-person examination of mental states, and it should by no means disqualify such introspective inquiry any more than the fact of observer-participancy has disqualified exploration in the field of quantum mechanics.

The fourth phase of this practice is the cultivation of mindfulness of mental objects, which include all non-intentional mental processes as well as all other kinds of phenomena that can be apprehended with the mind. Thus, this category is all-inclusive. At the same time, there is a special emphasis in this phase of practice on observing in oneself, others, and both oneself and others the contents of the mind affiliated with wholesome and unwholesome mental states, as well as the conditions leading to their emergence and dissolution. In addition, one mindfully observes all the phenomena of one's environment from one's own perspective by means of direct perception and from the perspective of others by means of imagination. The overarching theme of all these practices is the cultivation of a multi-perspectival view of oneself, others, and the inter-subjective relations between oneself and all other sentient beings. These techniques are explicitly designed to yield insights into these facets of the lived world, but they all have a strong bearing on the cultivation of compassion and other wholesome affective states, without which the cultivation of wisdom alone is said to be one more form of bondage.[8]

B. ALAN WALLACE began his studies of Tibetan Buddhism in 1970 at the University of Göttingen in Germany, and then continued his studies over the next fourteen years in India, Switzerland, and the United States. Ordained as a Buddhist monk by H. H. the Dalai Lama in 1975, he has taught Buddhist meditation and Buddhist philosophy worldwide since 1976 and has served as interpreter for numerous Tibetan scholars and contemplatives, including H. H. the Dalai Lama.

After graduating from Amherst College, where he studied physics and the philosophy of science, he returned his monastic vows and went on to earn his Ph.D. in religious studies at Stanford University. He then taught for four years in the Department of Religious Studies at the University

---

8 Excerpted with permission from his paper, "Intersubjectivity in Indo-Tibetan Buddhism."

of California at Santa Barbara, and is now the founder and president of the Santa Barbara Institute for Consciousness Studies (http://sbinstitute. com). His most recent books include *Mind in the Balance: Meditation in Science, Buddhism, and Christianity, Embracing Mind: The Common Ground of Science and Spirituality,* and *Hidden Dimensions: The Unification of Physics and Consciousness.*

THE PRACTICE OF
GIVING & RECEIVING

Acharya Judith Simmer-Brown

TONGLEN, LITERALLY 'SENDING AND TAKING,' is a Tibetan Buddhist contemplation practice for cultivating compassion. The great Indian master Atisha brought Tibetans this practice in the 11th-century, drawing from the powerful *Mahayana* or 'great vehicle' meditation traditions of India that taught the compassionate and wise path of the bodhisattvas, or 'beings dedicated to awakened heart.'

Tonglen meditation reverses the pattern of self-cherishing that is the knot of our personal suffering. Using breathing as the medium, *tonglen* awakens our hearts by opening us to those things we would rather avoid and encourages us to share what we would rather keep for ourselves. The practice shows that there are no real boundaries between living beings—we are all interdependent.

TONGLEN PRACTICE INSTRUCTIONS

We begin *tonglen* by taking our seats in sitting meditation with good posture, very simply and naturally. It is important to rest our minds in calm abiding *(shamatha)*. After a brief sitting period, we reflect on why we would want to do *tonglen?* Fundamentally, it is vast and choiceless. We recognize that we cannot practice for ourselves alone, as there is no private happiness. We are inextricably connected and involved with all beings, and we recognize that we all have, at core, awakened potential. The purpose of our human life is to grow larger hearts and more open minds, and we celebrate that we can do this in this moment. We are ready for transformation. Affirming this motivation begins the practice.

Then we become aware of our breathing, in and out, and establish the flow of the practice. On the in-breath, we breathe in thinking, "heavy, hot, dark," and on the out-breath, we breathe out thinking, "light, bright, cool." At first, it seems only like words, but it is good to develop a literal sense of this, with dark air moving into our nostrils and light air blowing out. My teacher, the Vidyadhara Trungpa Rinpoche, suggested that we think of ourselves as air-conditioners. We breathe in the stale, smoky, fetid air of the room around us, and we breathe out fresh, clean, cool air. Gradually, we purify the room. When we breathe, we are breathing with every pore of our bodies—in with "heavy, hot, dark," and out with "light, bright, cool." Do this for roughly one-third of the 20-minute session, or until the texture is established.

Next, we breathe with a continuing sense of the texture we have established. But now we open our thoughts and emotions to all of our personal material. It is good to start with beings who spontaneously arouse our compassion. Who do we know who is sick or in emotional turmoil? We begin visualizing that person's face before us, and breathe in their heavy, thick and hot suffering, sharing with them our own light, bright and cool energy. Be quite tangible with the texture. Whatever suffering you see in them, breathe it in; whatever sanity and kindness you see in yourself, you breathe it out to them.

When we are ready, extend beyond our loved ones to more difficult people or scenarios. Who or what do we see as threatening, or as problematic in our lives? We allow their faces or those scenarios to come to us, and then breathe in whatever suffering we encounter and extend out our sanity and kindness. It is important that we keep this personal, working with recent pain as well as old, familiar pain. We are practicing embracing what we would normally avoid, and sharing what we would normally hoard. Do this part of the practice for seven to ten minutes.

We conclude the practice by extending it out beyond our familiar world. One way to do this is to move geographically. We begin in our immediate neighborhood, with the family next door with the two babies, the college student on the other side who takes terrible care of her lawn, to the elderly woman across the street who recently lost her husband. Breathe in whatever pain we have experienced in them or in relation to them. Breathe out kindness, wakefulness. We move to those people we encounter on our daily routines—our co-workers and our boss; the grocery checker and stocker; the employees at the cleaners, the gas station, the drugstore. Then we extend through our community, to the hospital, the shelter, the jail, the nursing home, including everyone suffering there. Gradually, we extend to our state, region, country and world, our minds going to the painful situations there described in the newspaper—the wars, famines, epidemics. We also include the CEO's, the political leaders, and the people of privilege. We extend this practice until the twenty-minute session is over.

At the end of our *tonglen* session, it is important to return to calm abiding (*shamatha* meditation) practice, to let go of any agenda or feelings we have developed doing the practice. Just place mindfulness on breathing, let go of thoughts or emotions, keep good posture and let the mind settle into its own natural state.

WORKING WITH OBSTACLES

One of the most common obstacles to arise in *tonglen* practice is forgetfulness or numbness. It is threatening to our habitual patterns to do a practice that reverses our self-cherishing. We might even find ourselves falling asleep the moment we begin the practice. There are two ways of relating with this kind of obstacle. First, view the numbness or forgetfulness as the "heavy, hot, dark" part of our experience that we would rather not touch and breathe it in. Then breathe out the care and concern for others and the desire to help them. Then the obstacle becomes part of the practice.

The second antidote to numbness is to more openly expose ourselves to suffering off the cushion. Read the newspaper with an eye to *tonglen* subjects—war in Afghanistan, domestic violence in our town, reports of unemployment or scandal—all kindle in us desire to help. Then, the next time we are on the cushion, we have fresh material for *tonglen* and it becomes more natural to stay awake for it.

We also might be afraid that such a practice might make us sick. Surely it can't be good for us to breathe in suffering?! This is not the experience of seasoned meditators, who find that this practice is profoundly healing in body and mind. Breathing in pain begins to dissolve the barriers we erect to keep others away from us, and dissolving those barriers opens our hearts in profound ways. We begin to feel free of the fear that has dogged us most of our lives.

One way to make sure the practice works properly, however, is to make sure that we are not holding on to the heavy, hot, dark material we are taking in. We breathe in, and alchemically our awareness and care turn the painful material into wakefulness for ourselves and others. Breathe in fully—then breathe out fully, completing the cycle. This will ease our fear of imagined dangers of the practice.

We also may fear that we cannot handle the intensifying of emotion we imagine this practice brings. We are sure that opening in this way will make us neurotic messes. Ironically, the experience of this practice teaches us to feel emotions directly for a moment and then let them go. Usually we are afraid of feeling emotions, but opening with *tonglen* practice allows us to feel more deeply, but just for a moment. The fluidity of the practice builds greater depth and greater joy, as we 'touch and go' with intense emotionality.

We also may feel we have nothing to give, that it is impossible to 'send out' anything that is light, bright, or cool. Even our aspiration to help is something positive, so that if we feel that now we have nothing to give, our gift of a kind wish is a powerful thing. We can find something beneficial—visualizing a warm hug, a kind word, or empathetic heart. As we continue the practice, our confidence grows that there is always something beneficial to give to suffering people and situations.

Do we really help others this way? Of course, it takes time for us to be of benefit, but we can begin to witness subtle changes in how we relate to others. We do not react in anger or aversion, and we feel presence and empathy when we encounter their sufferings. This means we are available to others when they need us to be there. This is a tremendous help.

ALWAYS A CHANCE TO HELP

Tonglen practice is one of the most practical methods of transformation in Tibetan Buddhist traditions of meditation. Because it does not rely on empowerments, ritual implements, mantras, or specific places or times to practice, it can be practiced by anyone who truly feels the desire and responsibility to be of benefit to others. However, it is always helpful to have personal guidance with such a practice. Consider finding an experienced guide for your *tonglen* practice in the person of a meditation instructor or *tonglen* teacher. The most important thing is to do the practice regularly, daily if possible. The best part is that we always have a chance to help others.

ACHARYA JUDITH SIMMER-BROWN, Ph.D., is professor of Buddhist studies at Naropa University in Boulder, Colorado, where she has taught since 1978. She began her practice with Zen master Shunryu Suzuki, Roshi, in 1971, and then took the Vidyadhara, Trungpa Rinpoche as her root teacher in 1974. She continues to study with Sakyong Mipham Rinpoche, head of the Shambhala Buddhist lineage, and serves as the Dean of the Teachers' Academy for Shambhala International.

She teaches meditation practice, Buddhist philosophy and tantra, and participates in interreligious dialogues throughout North America, Europe, and Asia. She has also published widely in books, journals and periodicals on these topics. Her book, *Dakini's Warm Breath*, explores the feminine principle as it reveals itself in meditation practice and everyday life for women and men. Her most recent book, with Fran Grace, is an edited collection of articles called *Meditation in the Classroom: Contemplative Pedagogy for Religious Studies*. She and her husband, Richard Brown, have two children.

Christian Practices

FINDING INTIMACY WITH GOD

Father Thomas Keating

CENTERING PRAYER is a method of silent prayer that is designed to deepen our relationship with Christ and to prepare us to receive the gift of contemplative prayer, prayer in which we experience God's presence within us, closer than our very breath, closer than our thoughts, closer than consciousness itself; it is both a relationship with God and a discipline to foster that relationship.

The method itself was developed by Father William Meninger in the mid-1970's and based on indications from the anonymous Christian spiritual classic, The Cloud of Unknowing. Today it is practiced by people all over the world and spread through the work of Contemplative Outreach. Centering Prayer is not meant to replace other kinds of prayer; it simply adds depth of meaning to them, and to our daily lives. Centering Prayer is a movement beyond conversation with Christ to communion with Him, to a silent resting in His loving Presence.

THE METHOD OF CENTERING PRAYER

1. Choose a sacred word as the symbol of your intention to consent to God's presence and action within.

This word expresses our intention to be in God's presence and to yield to the divine action. It should be chosen during a brief period of prayer asking the Holy Spirit to inspire us with one that is especially suitable for us. Examples of this word might be: 'Lord,' 'Jesus,' 'Abba,' 'Father,' 'Mother,' or even, 'Love,' 'Peace,' 'Shalom,' or 'Silence.' Whatever word you choose, it should be used for the entire period of prayer.

2. Sitting comfortably and with eyes closed, settle briefly, and silently introduce the sacred word as the symbol of your consent to God's presence and action within.

"Sitting comfortably" does not mean that we are so comfortable that we might fall asleep, but just comfortable enough to avoid thinking about the discomfort of our bodies during prayer. Keeping one's back straight is an important part of proper posture for Centering Prayer. We also close our eyes in this process to let go of what is going on around us. For it is into this withdrawal from the senses that we introduce the sacred word, as gently as laying a feather on a piece of absorbent cotton.

3. When you become aware of being engaged with your thoughts, return ever-so-gently to the sacred word.

"Thoughts" may refer to any perception, including sense perceptions, feelings, images, memories, reflections, and commentaries. It is normal for these perceptions to arise, but still we should remember to return "ever-so-gently to the sacred word," using the minimum of effort. This is the only activity we initiate during the time of Centering Prayer. However, during the course of your prayer, you may notice that the sacred word is becoming vague or even disappearing. Do not worry; this is simply part of the process of Centering Prayer.

4. At the end of the prayer period, remain in silence with eyes closed for two or three minutes.

If this prayer is done in a group, the leader may slowly recite the "Our Father" during the additional two or three minutes while the others listen. The additional two or three minutes give the psyche time to readjust to the external senses and enable us to bring the atmosphere of silence into daily life.

It should be noted that the principal effects of Centering Prayer are experienced in daily life, not in the period of Centering Prayer itself.

The minimum time for this prayer is about twenty minutes. Two periods are recommended each day, one first thing in the morning, and one in the afternoon or early evening.

The end of the prayer period can be indicated by a timer, provided it does not have an audible tick or loud sound when it goes off.

Various physical irritations may be noticed during your prayer. These may include slight pains, itches, or twitches in various parts of the body, or a generalized restlessness. These are usually due to the untying of emotional knots in the body. You may also notice heaviness or lightness in the extremities. This is usually due to a deep level of spiritual attentiveness. In either case, pay no attention to them, or simply allow the mind to rest briefly in the sensation and then return to the sacred word.

FATHER THOMAS KEATING (b. 1923), is a Cistercian monk and former abbot of St. Joseph's Abbey in Spencer, Massachusetts, where he, along with Father William Meninger and Father Basil Pennington, first developed the technique of Centering Prayer. He is also the founder of Contemplative Outreach, the Snowmass Interreligious Conference, and a former president of the Temple of Understanding. The author of numerous books and articles on Christian contemplative practice, including *Open Mind, Open Heart, Manifesting God,* and *Divine Therapy & Addiction,* Father Keating is one of the foremost experts on the contemplative dimensions of Christian spirituality, and one of the most revered elders of the world's spiritual community. He currently resides at St. Benedict's Monastery in Snowmass, Colorado.

Making the Soul Fertile

Father David Denny

MANY CHRISTIAN MEDITATION practices have emerged over the centuries and across schools of Christian spirituality. Exploring this long and wide territory, we can distill some basic tenets about what is generally known as 'discursive meditation' or *meditatio* in Christianity. By 'discourse,' we mean the use of words, thoughts or images. 'Meditation,' however, is a more difficult term to define and describe. In my own practice, I find it helpful to locate meditation between spiritual reading *(lectio divina)* and prayer. Prayer itself may be active, as in the active expression of desire, sorrow, bafflement, thanksgiving: the panoply of human emotion and the wondering perplexity of our limited intellect. It is the radical response of the created *I* to the uncreated *Thou.* Or, as prayer matures, it tends to become more passive and receptive, quieter, darker, simpler, without method and pervasive: a fertile desert. We believe that, essentially, in the deeper transformative sense, we cannot pray. Rather, God initiates true prayer. All we can do is prepare ourselves. And that's what meditation does. God plants the seed. Meditation prepares the ground, the soil of the soul. Meditation is like making compost out of the raw ingredients of our broken lives. It makes humus. And this *hum-ility* makes us vulnerable to insemination by what early Christian sages called the *logos spermatikos,* the 'seed-word,' the "grain of wheat" that dies and germinates new, eternal life.[9]

A MEASURED APPROACH

Our English word meditate comes from a root that means *healing*, as in 'medicine' and *harmony*, as in 'modal' or 'commodious.' It also means *appropriately measured*, as in 'moderate.' Not mediocre, but in touch with and exposed to extremes while anchored, so that

9 John 12:24.

extreme weather cannot sweep us away into a shipwreck. That's why the early monastics were called anchorites. Meditation heals and harmonizes what the Christian tradition understands as our two fundamental human acts: *knowing* and *loving*.

Another way to approach meditation is to call it a method for cultivating the fruits of Baptism and Eucharist. These central rituals of the Christian tradition impart objective, saving grace. But if we make no effort to make good soil—*a humble soul*— then the 'seed-word' may soon shrivel.[10] We may continue going to church, but our participation in ritual becomes sterile, hypocritical or superstitious ritualism—fruitless—and our Christianity may become its opposite—an ideology prone to violence and exclusivism.

Because discourse implies thinking, words and images, we need to examine the Christian understanding of language, symbol and the five senses. Because of the Incarnation (the teaching that God became human in Jesus), we may not consider words, images, flesh, blood, time and space as profane. They are not distractions from some ethereal realm. They are allusions, not illusions. They are sacramental: they may veil, but they also reveal. They are icons, not idols. That's why, in the Roman Catholic, Orthodox, and other liturgical Christian traditions, we use lots of 'smells and bells' in our liturgies. We take 'appropriate measures' in approaching the immense.

In this regard, discursive meditation is 'sensuous.' We may distinguish between sensuous reverent affirmation of creation, and sensual abuse of the body resulting often from an unhealed wound. Meditation, along with appropriate therapy when necessary, may be a means to healing our senses. "Only a soul that has been made pure," according to French writer Paul Claudel, "will understand the fragrance of the rose," or the meaning of scripture. This sacramental vision has been called the *cataphatic* approach to meditation and prayer, the *via positiva,* or the way of affirmation.

TRADITIONAL TEACHINGS

What clues does the Christian tradition give us about the practice of meditation? According to the 12th century Carthusian monk Guigo II, "Meditation is the busy application of the mind to seek

---

10 Luke 8:12-14.

with the help of one's own reason for knowledge of hidden truth." It "considers . . . carefully what is to be sought after" in spiritual reading; "it digs, as it were, for the treasure which it finds and reveals, but since it is not in meditation's power to seize upon the treasure, it directs us to prayer." After a careful reading of a passage from Scripture, the meditator mulls over the reading, seeking the 'hidden' or mystical meaning of the literal words. Medieval monks referred to this as 'rumination,' chewing on the words to extract the nutrients, the trace elements that may increase the fertility of our minds and hearts. It is not information we seek, but guidance and illumination. How does this passage of scripture speak to *me*? After all, as the letter to the Hebrews puts it, "the word of God is living and active and sharper than any two-edged sword . . ."[11]

As we meditate we are aware only of the mental activity and discipline that keeps us focused on the 'treasure hunt.' But our faith allows us to trust that more is taking place: the Spirit acts as an end cause, a hidden magnetic force drawing us passively, even as we are consciously, actively engaged in reflecting on a scene from scripture. For example, imagine being one of the heartbroken disciples of Jesus who hears Peter announce that he's going fishing in order to distract himself from his grief and sense of failure:[12]

> I spend a long, silent, fruitless night on the lake. Instead of escaping my grief, the silent lapping of the water on the side of the boat, the careless stars and the rhythmic rocking only allow the grief to sink more deeply into my bones. Loneliness increases. I second-guess myself: "How could I have run away when he was arrested? And why did he allow them to take him away without resisting? I miss him. I miss the sound of his voice . . . No one laughed as he did! He seemed so free, humble and vulnerable; yes, but he seemed so alive, with a life that could never be snuffed out."
>
> Morning breaks, and out of the melancholy grayness comes a voice from shore telling Peter to cast his net again. No one tells Peter how to fish! But Peter has, for the moment at least, lost some of his old fight, so he complies.
>
> We're swamped! The nets should break with the weight of the haul. Then John says something crazy: "It is the Lord!"

11 Hebrew 4:12.
12 John 21:3.

We look at each other, stunned. I think: "Poor John. He still can't face it."

But then "Mr. Practicality" himself, Peter, ever the sober blue-collar no-nonsense man, gasps as if he's seen or heard a ghost. He does the strangest thing. Instead of throwing himself into the lake as he used to do, he throws on his clothes first and then leaps into the dawn waters. I honestly thought both Peter and John had snapped. But I also felt something stir in me when I heard that voice from the shore, and a hope I had spent the night burying began to stir disturbingly inside me.

Still, we manned the oars mostly in order to pluck Peter out of the water before he sank, dragged down by the weight of his extra clothes. But he was driven by some preternatural burst of energy and we weren't far from shore, so we hit the shallows quickly. Then I looked up. The man behind the voice from shore was impossible. John's madness could not have produced this phantom. The body I had seen wasted, drained of blood and life only days before, stood there in his familiar way, with a twinkle in his eye as the morning sun hit his face. He seemed genuinely glad to see me. The horror I felt for a moment, recollecting how I had abandoned him and anticipating his anger, fled. I will never forget that moment. It remains as a kind of scar, an intuition of hell. Then that mischievous smile, and the simple greeting, "Good morning, friends. What's for breakfast?" It was heaven on earth.

This is just one example of how we might be drawn into an encounter with the living Christ through discursive meditation. St. Ignatius of Loyola proposes another approach. A former soldier, Ignatius used military imagery in his *Spiritual Exercises*. He suggests we consider ourselves soldiers in Satan's army. He describes how Satan operates, how he treats his soldiers, and his strategy for conquering the world. Then Ignatius asks us to consider what it would be like to be a soldier in Jesus' army of humility. How does *he* treat *his* soldiers? What is their goal? It is well worth reading, both as a meditation and as a literary work.

Even a puritanical saint like Bernard of Clairvaux spoke positively of the role of imagination and symbols in meditation. In Sermon 41 on the Song of Songs, Bernard reflects on the meaning of a pair of earrings that the Bride of the Song of Songs is about to receive. In Christian spirituality, heaven is understood primarily in terms of seeing. We say that in heaven we will enjoy the "Beatific Vision." For now, we must make do with hearing as our deepest sense: "Faith comes through hearing," according to St. Paul.[13] Still, angels approach the Bride's ears to bestow earrings of gold and silver. "I cannot see what this may mean," writes Bernard . . .

> if not the construction of certain spiritual images in order to bring the purest intuition of divine wisdom before the eyes of the soul that contemplates, to enable it to perceive, as through puzzling reflections in a mirror, what it cannot possibly gaze on as yet face to face . . . when the spirit is ravished out of itself and granted a vision of God that suddenly shines into the mind with the swiftness of a lightning-flash, immediately, but whence I know not, images of earthly things fill the imagination, either as an aid to understanding or to temper the intensity of the divine light. So well-adapted are they to the divinely illuminated senses, that in their shadow the utterly pure and brilliant radiance of the truth is rendered more bearable to the mind and more capable of being communicated to others.

These "puzzling reflections," Bernard speculates, are "fashioned . . . by angelic hands from pure and beautiful images, which I feel bring us in contact somehow with the being of God . . ." Although as we noted earlier we may only be aware of focusing our attention on an image found in our reading, we may be drawn imperceptibly by angelic presences to insights and perceptions our natural faculties neither create nor fully comprehend.

DAILY DISCIPLINE

In order for meditation to fulfill its goal of readying us for prayer, we need to practice it at least once daily. Experiment with different times of day and length of time. If you're an early riser, you will likely do best first thing, before other responsibilities take hold of your attention. If you are a night owl, you may find the quiet night hour before sleep an appropriate time. Don't bite off more than you can chew. You may begin with ten minutes. As you continue, you

13 Romans 10:17.

will likely expand the amount of time. Traditionally, we begin with reading scripture but feel free to expand the possibilities. You may find a spiritual writer or poet whose work speaks to you on a deep level. You don't need a lot of words. In fact, the fewer the better. You may prefer to look at a painting or photograph. Then close your eyes and allow yourself to ruminate, chewing on the words or image, allowing the 'text' to sink into your heart. Keep your book open, and if you find your mind wandering, reread the passage that spoke to you, and return to your reflection. Don't worry or accuse yourself of being scatterbrained. It's a great opportunity to practice patience with the chattering mind and to exercise gently the muscles of focused attention.

In the beginning stages, you may feel you are regressing. Don't worry. You are probably simply becoming more aware of how little mental discipline you have. It's humbling, but this awareness is a sign of progress. Over time, your method may simplify. You may read less. You may use fewer images. You may feel a need to supplement your cataphatic practice with Centering Prayer. You may find certain compulsions begin to dissipate. Or, if you continue to suffer from certain compulsive thought patterns or behaviors that you wish to change, you may benefit from other therapeutic help. Therapy, combined with a discipline of meditation, will likely accelerate your healing. You may find yourself entering a desert or wilderness that feels empty, yet spacious and liberating. Discourse, images and symbols have done their work. And as Christ continues to take flesh in the community of mercy, justice and love he initiated, so we return again to words, images, and symbols that bloom from the desert and speak anew to our hearts. "The wilderness and the desert will be glad, and the desert will rejoice and blossom."[14]

FATHER DAVE DENNY is a Christian hermit in the tradition of the desert mothers and fathers. After spending time as an exchange student in Afghanistan and studying Middle Eastern History and Arabic at the University of Arizona, Father Dave joined the Spiritual Life Institute, radically experimental Carmelite monastic community in Sedona, Arizona in 1975. He was ordained to the priesthood in the community in 1980, and served as co-editor of *Desert Call,* the quarterly magazine of the Spiritual Life Institute from 1985-2004.

14 Isaiah 35:1.

In 2005, Father Dave left the Spiritual Life Institute to fully embrace the eremitical life as a desert father *(abba),* and to co-found The Desert Foundation with fellow hermit, Tessa Bielecki. The Desert Foundation (www. sandandsky.org) is an informal circle of friends who wish to explore the spiritual wisdom of the desert with a special focus on peace and understanding between the three Abrahamic traditions: Judaism, Christianity and Islam.

From 1993-2011, Father Dave was a visiting professor at Colorado College, teaching "Fire and Light: A History of Christian Mysticism," and from 2007-2011, "Sand and Sky: Desert Spirituality from the Middle East to the American Southwest." In 2013, he co-authored *Season of Glad Songs: A Christmas Anthology* with Tessa Bielecki. An essayist and poet, Father Dave's writing now appears on-line in Sand and Sky: Desert Voices (www.sandandsky.org). He currently lives in a hermitage in Crestone, Colorado, though he frequently serves as a chaplain for Image Journal's Glen Workshop, as well as for Seattle Pacific University's MFA spring residencies.

THE ANGELUS —
A MINDFULNESS PRACTICE

Tessa Bielecki

YOU MAY HEAR BELLS ringing from Roman Catholic churches around your neighborhood at 6 am, high noon, and 6 pm. They resound in a distinctive rhythm: three bells, three bells, three, and nine. This is an ancient prayer tradition known as the 'Angelus.' Many Catholics call it a 'Marian devotion,' but I consider it a vibrant mindfulness practice.

We do not know how old this tradition is, nor when it was first named the Angelus, after the opening words. Its beginnings may go back over a thousand years. This devotion is an integral part of monastic life. More importantly, it is part of the daily devotional life of millions of householders everywhere around the world.

THE STORY

The meditation recalls the moment when Gabriel, the Angel of the Lord, *Angelus Domini* in Latin (hence, 'Angelus'), appeared to the Virgin Mary and announced that she would become the Mother of God and bear Jesus into the world. You can read the full tale in the first chapter of the Gospel of Luke, the only evangelist who tells the story. This sacred event is called the 'Annunciation,' commemorated annually in a major Church feast on March 25, nine months to the day before Christmas. And we commemorate the Annunciation every day, three times a day, at the hours of the Angelus.

This event has been a frequent theme throughout the history of Christian art, painted by Michelangelo, Botticelli, Leonardo da Vinci, Simone Martini and others. In these Renaissance paintings, Gabriel assumes the traditional male and winged form. He is splendidly clothed in beautiful robes and kneels before the Virgin.

Mary usually bows her head, crosses her arms across her chest, and holds a lily, symbol of her purity.

My favorite Angelus art is more contemporary, painted by African-American artist Henry O. Tanner in 1898. Tanner left Philadelphia in 1891 because of racism and moved to France, where he lived for the rest of his life. He also visited the Middle East in order to make his many biblical paintings more accurate. In Tanner's vivid account of the Annunciation, Mary sits among her crumpled bed sheets, almost cowering in the corner of her room, yet tilting her head up and towards the angel. Gabriel takes no definite shape but is instead more appropriately represented by light or energy. Earlier painters portrayed a Mary immediately willing, perhaps even subservient. Tanner's rendition is truer to the Gospel story.

According to Luke, Gabriel greets Mary: "Rejoice, highly favored one, the Lord is with you; blessed are you among women." But Mary is "troubled" and even fearful, wondering what this can possibly mean. So the angel has to reassure her: "Do not be afraid, Mary, for you have found favor with God." This is relevant to the Angelus practice, for we are often troubled, questioning, or afraid when we hear the bells ring.

THE WORDS

The Angelus is easily recited alone but even more powerful when recited with one or two others 'antiphonally,' that is, back and forth in different voices. At the first three bells you say: "The Angel of the Lord declared unto Mary." The response is: "And she conceived of the Holy Spirit." You follow with a Hail Mary: "Hail Mary, full of grace, the Lord is with you. Blessed are you among women, and blessed is the fruit of your womb, Jesus. Holy Mary, Mother of God, pray for us sinners, now and at the hour of our death. Amen."

At the second set of three bells you pray: "Behold the handmaid of the Lord." And the response is: "Be it done unto me according to your word." Another Hail Mary follows. At the third set of bells you continue: "And the Word became Flesh." The response: "And dwelt among us." And a third Hail Mary follows.

During the final nine bells you conclude: "Pray for us, O holy Mother of God, that we may be made worthy of the promises of

Christ." And then: "Pour forth, we beseech you, O Lord, your grace into our hearts, that we to whom the Incarnation of Christ your Son was made known by the message of an angel, may by his passion and cross be brought to the glory of his resurrection, through the same Christ our Lord. Amen."

THE HISTORY

According to Brother David Steindl-Rast, an Austrian Benedictine monk steeped in earthy Roman Catholic devotional practices even longer than I, the evening Angelus bell is the most ancient of the three and goes back to the time of the Crusades, one of the few positive elements of that sad era in Christian history. It was at first a signal to extinguish all fires for safety at night. (This is the origin of our word 'curfew,' which means to 'cover the fire.') And the Angelus bells reminded the faithful to pray for the Crusaders so far from home.

The morning bell originated in the medieval monasteries. Christians in the neighborhood joined the monks in three Hail Marys when they heard the monastery bells for Lauds, the monastic prayer at dawn. The noon bell rang at first only on Fridays, in memory of Christ's crucifixion. Around the time that Columbus set sail on the Niña, the Pinta, and the Santa Maria, the noon-day bell was also rung daily as a special reminder to pray for world peace. Soon after that, the Angelus evolved into the form we know today.

Brother David describes the "inner cogency" in this development. Many other religious traditions single out morning, noon, and nightfall as special times of prayer. "Even the birds mark sunrise and sunset with their singing and high noon with a silence that carries its own relevant message," he says. I am writing this reflection for you by Oak Creek in the high desert of Sedona, Arizona, as the cicadas begin their Evensong and the sun sets behind the red sandstone monoliths.

The Meaning

How is the Angelus a valuable mindfulness practice? When the bells begin to ring, you completely stop whatever you're doing and attend to the prayer. St. Benedict told his monks not to dot an *i* or cross a *t!* This means that you stop and pray, or stop and consider, when it is time, not only when you feel like praying.

'Stop and consider' is a good definition of true prayer, which goes far beyond 'saying prayers.' So is 'singling things out for grateful consideration.' Another definition I learned early in my own years of monastic life is this: "Prayer is moving into a promise and relying on it." Notice how part of the Angelus speaks of the "promises of Christ," not glibly, but in terms of our worthiness. The real wonder is that receiving the blessing of the promise does not actually rely on our worthy performance but on the gratuitous mercy of God!

'Mindfulness' is a term I first heard from my Buddhist friends, and I have learned much from it. But the word is sometimes too cold and abstract for me. I prefer the phrase "personal passionate presence." In the Jewish Testament (the Hebrew Bible), God often speaks to major biblical figures, calling out to them personally and passionately from the fullness of his presence. So William McNamara, my first teacher in the Carmelite tradition, claims that we can actually call God "Personal Passionate Presence." This is my favorite description of God. (When people ask me what my own experience of God is like, I always answer, "Presence.")

Personal Passionate Presence

In Genesis, the first book of the Bible, God calls out to Adam, "O Man, where art thou?" And Adam, which means 'man,' answers, "Here I am, Lord." This same scenario of call and response is repeated throughout the Jewish Testament. When you look at the stories, you see that the real response is not a verbal statement of presence, but a full-bodied existential *instance* of presence. Adam's every word embodies his whole response: "Here I am," personally passionately present myself to your Personal Passionate Presence.

This is the deepest meaning of the Angelus prayer for me. No matter how mindless or scattered we may be by the circumstances of any given day, when the Angelus bells ring, we have the opportunity to gather together the fragments of our being, come back to center, and experience ourselves as fully present in the moment. As Ram Dass so wisely put it decades ago, we can "be here now."

Jean-François Millet (1814-1875) depicted this beautifully in his painting, *L'Angelus*. Two peasants stand in a field where they have been digging potatoes. They are flanked by a pitchfork, a basket, and a wheelbarrow full of burlap bags. In the distance we see the tiny spire of the village church and can almost hear the bells ring. The man and woman bow their heads, the woman folding her hands, the man holding his hat. We can almost hear their sighs as they stop their hard work, rest for a moment, consider who they are, who God is, and come back to themselves and what is most important in their lives. The colors of the painting are muted and bright at the same time: the sky pink and grey (is it dawn or dusk?), the background field deep green, the harvested field in the foreground rich autumnal gold and brown. The woman's cap and sleeves sing out in vivid red. Millet shows this man and woman truly in the moment, living on the spot where they are, personally and passionately present, only here, only now.

I must confess that I pray the Angelus less often and more informally now that I am no longer a monk. Since I live alone in a solitary log cabin in the middle of the vast and arid San Luis Valley in southern Colorado, there are no bells anywhere around to remind me to 'stop and consider.' So it's more challenging to remember the formally appointed Angelus times. The rhythms of the sun, the moon, and the stars, rising over the Sangre de Cristo Mountains and setting over the San Juans, are stronger and more natural reminders for me to be personally and passionately present in the here and now, singling out aspects of my life for grateful consideration.

I have prayed the Angelus for almost fifty years, alone and with others, in the monastery, the city, the oceans of my childhood, the deserts of Arizona, the woods of Nova Scotia, the mountains of Colorado, and the rocky green fields of Ireland, in the midst of cooking in the kitchen, weeding in the garden, cutting or stacking firewood. A ritual like the Angelus, repeated daily and over the years, grows richer and richer as memories begin to cling to it "like lichens to ancient rocks or lavender fragrance to an old chest," as Brother David once wrote. May your own life be blessed and enriched by this simple practice.

Tessa Bielecki is a Christian hermit in the tradition of the desert mothers and fathers. Co-founder of the Spiritual Life Institute, she was a Carmelite monk and Mother Abbess for almost 40 years, establishing radically experimental monastic communities of men and women in Arizona,

Colorado, Nova Scotia, and Ireland. For all of that time, she was also the editor-in-chief of *Desert Call,* the quarterly magazine of the Spiritual Life Institute. In the 1980s, Tessa was actively involved in the groundbreaking Buddhist-Christian dialogues at Naropa University, an experience that proved pivotal in her life, opening her up to the wisdom of many other spiritual paths.

In 2005, she left the Spiritual Life Institute to fully embrace the eremitical life as a desert mother *(amma),* and to co-found The Desert Foundation with fellow hermit, Father Dave Denny. The Desert Foundation (www.sandandsky.org) is an informal circle of friends who wish to explore the spiritual wisdom of the desert with a special focus on peace and understanding between the three Abrahamic traditions: Judaism, Christianity and Islam.

Tessa is the author of several critically acclaimed books on Teresa of Avila, including: *Holy Daring: An Outrageous Gift to Modern Spirituality from Saint Teresa, the Wild Woman of Avila; Teresa of Avila: Mystical Writings;* and *Teresa of Avila: Ecstasy and Common Sense.* She recently co-authored (with Father Dave Denny) a new collection of writings on the Christmas season, *Season of Glad Songs.* Her audio recordings include: *Wild at Heart: Radical Teachings of the Christian Mystics,* and *Teresa of Avila: The Book of My Life.* Tessa currently lives in a hermitage in Crestone, Colorado, though she continues to teach on Christian mysticism and the contemplative life at retreats and workshops around the world.

Hindu Practices

THE BREATH
WITHIN THE BREATH

Yogi Nataraja Kallio

A STUDENT ONCE ASKED Kabir, one of India's most beloved poets and mystics, "Where is God to be found?" Kabir replied, "He is the breath within the breath." This famous utterance intimates how something as seemingly simple as the breath can be a doorway to connecting with Ultimate Reality.

In the Yoga tradition, breath practice is called *pranayama,* and is considered an essential tool not only for creating health and harmony in the body, but also for the expansion of consciousness and the realization of our true nature. The word, *pranayama* is comprised of two words: *prana,* 'life-force' or 'energy,' and *ayama,* 'expansion' or 'extension.' Though often thought of as a therapeutic practice, the deeper aim of *pranayama* is to purify, free and expand the energy of body and mind. For *pranayama* uses the physical breath to access and create change in the subtle breath or life-force.

According to Yoga philosophy, all experience is born of two fundamental principles: *prana,* 'life-force' and *chitta,* 'consciousness.' All that we experience—from the most manifest and dense to the most refined and subtle—is an expression of life-force, whereas that which experiences it is consciousness. Like two dancers moving in unison, these two principles are intimately related; a movement in one creates a reciprocal movement in the other. The *Hatha Yoga Pradipika* describes this relationship in the following way: "When *prana* moves, *chitta* moves. When *prana* is without movement, *chitta* is without movement." Thus, by moving our breath consciously, we can create an immediate shift in our state of mind.

Yoga practitioners believe that our subtle body is composed of numerous streams of life-force, called *nadis* in Sanskrit. Of these, the *sushumna nadi*, the 'hollow reed' is of greatest importance. Situated along the central axis of the body, it is considered the central current of intelligence from which all the peripheral *nadis* radiate, and into which they absorb in moments of illumination. The *sushumna nadi*, which is also described as the 'staff of God,' the 'path of liberation,' and the 'pillar of light,' is the energetic correlate to non-dual awareness and the circuitry by which the divine force manifests in our life.

Indicating the importance of the *sushumna nadi* in Yogic practice, the culminating verse of the *Hatha Yoga Pradipika* states: "Until the *prana* has entered the *sushumna nadi* and the mind has assumed the form of *Brahman* (the Divine), all this talk of wisdom and knowledge is nothing but the nonsensical babbling of a madman."

From earth to heaven, the *sushumna nadi* can be sensed during moments of sincere prayer and aspiration as an ascending current of expansion. From heaven to earth, the *sushumna nadi* can be felt in moments of receptivity and surrender, as a current of grace, descending and integrating into one's being.

The ultimate intention of most *pranayama* practices, including the one described below, is to purify, awaken and unite the pranic force with the *sushumna nadi*, thereby impelling the peripheral or individual self to unite with the supreme Self.

THE FULL YOGIC BREATH:

DISCOVERING THE BREATH WITHIN THE BREATH

The Full Yogic Breath is made up of four components, which, when practiced together, help us to unite mind and the life-force with the *sushumna nadi*.

1. Posture

The first component of the practice is posture. Like a mountain, whether seated on the ground or in a chair, the body must be upright, still and relaxed. This allows the spine of the physical body to be free from obstruction so that the subtle body can be felt without distraction.

Once seated in a fully upright and relaxed position, firmly root the sitting bones and slightly recoil the pelvic floor (perineum) towards the heart. This gesture is called *mulabandha* in Sanskrit and moves the pelvic force upwards towards the heart.[15]

2. Ujjayi Pranayama

The second component of the practice involves beginning to move the breath consciously through *ujjayi pranayama*, the 'upward moving, victorious breath.'

While breathing through the nose, slightly constrict the back of the throat (the glottis muscle), as if you were swallowing something. This narrows the passage through which the breath passes, which in turn lengthens the duration of the breath, as well as creating a soft, aspirate, whispering sound, similar to the sound of the ocean when heard from a distance.

This sound serves both as an anchor to focus the mind, as well as a mirror to reflect the relative smoothness, evenness and quality of the breath. For example, if the sound is loud at the beginning and soft or gasping at the end, it indicates that one is not breathing evenly. The aim is to breathe so that the sound is consistent from the inception to the end of the breath cycle.

3. Breathing the Entire Body

The third component of the practice involves lengthening the breath throughout the entire body, thereby mirroring the physical breath with the movement of the *sushumna nadi*.

The lungs can be divided into three sections: upper (upper torso and shoulders), middle (mid rib cage and heart), and lower (diaphragm to the middle ribs). The aim of the full Yogic breath is to breathe evenly through all three sections of the lungs.[16]

---

15 This practice can also be done lying down as long as the spine is straight and one can remain alert.

16 Hypertension, neglect, stress, depression, psychological repression all serve to narrow the breath capacity. As we become afflicted by external and psychological challenges, it is a common response to shorten the breath, breathing only through a limited section of the lungs. This results in a host of maladies such as oxygen deprivation, increased carbon dioxide build up and nervous and mental tension. If nothing else, it is essential to learn abdominal breathing (breathing into the lower lungs which causes the belly to swell on the inhalation and retract on the exhalation) as the majority of oxygen receptors reside in the floor of the lungs, and the parasympathetic nervous system is stimulated.

Though the physical breath is limited to the lungs, in this *pranayama*, the focus is on the sensation of the breath, which stretches through the entire body. During inhalation the breath stretches from the lower lungs, through the middle lungs, to the upper lungs, like a cup being filled with water; however, the sensation of the inhalation stretches all the way down to the base of the body, rooting in the pelvic floor, while simultaneously rising upwards towards the crown of the head.

With the exhalation, the 'cup' empties, as the breath releases from upper lungs to lower lungs; however the sensation of the breath descends (without collapsing the chest), all the way to the base of the torso.

To assist in this practice keep the lowest wall of the abdomen slightly lifted and toned. This allows the sensation of the breath to simultaneously descend all the way to the pelvic floor and rise towards the crown, without being consumed by the otherwise inflating belly.

THE FOUR FUNCTIONS OF THE BREATH

There are four aspects within a *pranayama* breath cycle: inhalation *(puraka),* exhalation *(rechaka),* retention after inhalation *(antar kumbhaka),* and retention after exhalation *(bahir kumbhaka).* Each serves a unique function in effecting change in the physical, subtle, and mental body.

Inhalation: "Inhalation *(puraka)* is the intake of cosmic energy by the individual for his growth and progress. . . . It is the Infinite uniting with the finite. It draws in the breath of life as carefully and as gently as the fragrance of a flower might be indrawn and distributes it evenly throughout the body."[17]

Exhalation: "Exhalation is the outflow of the individual energy *(jivatma)* to unite with the cosmic energy *(Paramatma).* It quietens [sic.] and silences the brain. It is the surrender of the sadhaka's ego to and immersion in the Self."[18]

Retention: As the breath is stilled, the *prana* is stilled, enabling the mind to become still as well. It is essential to know that this is the most powerful part of *pranayama* and must be treated extremely delicately. Never hold the breath to the point of creating

17 B.K.S. Iyengar, Light on Pranayama: The Yogic Art of Breathing, 99.
18 Ibid., 100.

any strain or tension.

Integrating all of the above points, a good introductory inhalation, exhalation, and retention ratio might be: 4-2-6-1.

1. Inhale for the count of 4, feeling the sensation of the inhalation, like a tree, simultaneously rooting through the base of the body as it ascends towards the crown;

2. Hold the breath in for the count of 2, being still, pausing at the end of the inhalation;

3. Exhale for the count of 6, feeling the sensation of the breath descend, while keeping the heart open, the body upright;

4. Hold the breath out for the count of 1, feeling the empty stillness;

5. This completes one round. Continue for 9-27 rounds.

As this ratio becomes comfortable, you can slightly increase the duration of each phase of the breath. At no point should there be any strain, as this will create a strain in the nervous system and mind. If you experience any tightness or strain, reduce the ratio of the breath and let the practice become more effortless.

4. Meditation on the Pillar of Light

The fourth and final component of the Full Yogic Breath involves the attunement of the mind with the subtle body. As the breath becomes more conscious and expansive, align your awareness with the *sushumna nadi* by feeling the sensations along the central axis of the body. Allow your awareness to unite with this innermost stream on sensation, feeling yourself as a pillar of light.

Finally, after completing a number of breath cycles, let the technique dissolve on the exhalation, and simply abide as awareness itself, the space in which life-force spontaneously unfolds. This is the essence of *pranayama*, the gateway to the breath within the breath.

The full possibility of what this practice intends may not be discovered immediately but requires regular practice. Initially the practice is to simply discover the subtleties involved in freeing the breath to flow evenly through the entire body. When the physical components of this practice become effortless, the attunement to the 'breath within the breath,' the *sushumna nadi*, becomes more accessible and spontaneous, allowing for its integration into all aspects of one's life.

YOGI NATARAJA KALLIO, M.A., is head of Yoga Teacher Training in the Traditional Eastern Arts program at Naropa University in Boulder, Colorado. Nataraja has been a student of Yoga for over twenty years, seven of which were spent studying intensively in India. He has studied and practiced in the lineages of Sri Aurobindo, Purna Yoga, Swami Sivananda, Swami Satyananda, Swami Gitananda, Krishnamacharya (i.e., the Iyengar, Ashtanga, and Viniyoga schools), as well as the Tantric Sri Vidya tradition of South India. Nataraja has taught at Naropa University since 2000 and designed the Yoga Teacher Training concentration in 2006, which he has overseen ever since.

THE PRACTICE OF SELF-ENQUIRY

John Allen Grimes

IN SOME ADVAITA VEDANTA traditions[19] of Hinduism, Self-enquiry is not regarded as a meditation practice that takes place at certain hours and in certain positions. The practice of Self-enquiry of the 'I'-thought is a gentle technique that bypasses the usual repressive methods of controlling the mind. It is not an exercise in concentration or meditation, nor does it aim at suppressing thoughts. It merely invokes awareness of the source from which the mind, and thus all meditation techniques, spring.

To put into question the one who is asking the questions is to put into motion an enquiry that may end in the veritable destruction of the questioner. The consequences of this may not be, need not be, what they seem. The consequences need not entail the destruction of whom one really is, but merely the destruction of whom one *thinks* one is. You see, the meditator, meditating, is meditated. I, the meditator, think I, a distinct human being, am doing something, i.e., meditating. By meditating, I believe I am acting and employing a technique or method that is other than me. Meditated, in this context, is not a verb implying an action. It is a synonym for Reality, for that which is the ground and source of all, though itself, it does nothing. That is the mystery.

If my name is something that belongs to me, but is not an essential part of who I am, then am I my physical body? Obviously, the same logic holds good here too. The physical body is also something that belongs to me. We all say, "This is my body," "this is my hair," "these are my hands." But I am not my body, my hair, nor my hands, nor my gender, nor even the sum total of all these physical parts. Even a little reflection reveals that I could change my hair

---

19 The Sanskrit word, *advaita,* literally means, 'not-two.' Therefore, the philosophical school known as Advaita Vedanta affirms the non-duality of the Absolute or *Brahman,* the qualified reality of the empirical world, and the identity of the individual soul, or *jiva,* with *Brahman.* — Ed.

color or the shape of my nose (or my gender and so on), I would still remain *me*. A change of the mere surface appearance does not fundamentally, essentially, alter who I really am.

Then am I my thoughts? Thoughts come and go. Thoughts belong to me. The thoughts I had as a child are no longer my thoughts. Even as the body continually undergoes change, one's thoughts are continually changing. They come and go. They belong to me, but the one that they belong to does not change. Even a little reflection reveals that there must be an unchanging substratum to support, to maintain, that which is ever-changing. One's faculty of memory reveals that there must be something permanent which strings together the ever-changing.

Who am I? What is the best method of spiritual practice? That depends on the temperament of the individual. Every person is born with latent tendencies from his past lives. One method will prove easy to one person and another to another. There can be no general rule. There are numerous methods. You may practice Self-enquiry asking yourself: "Who am I?" or if that does not appeal to you, you may meditate on "I am *Brahman*," or some other theme; or you may concentrate on your breath, the light, an incarnation. The object in every case is to make the mind one-pointed, to concentrate it on one thought, and thereby exclude the many other thoughts. If one does this, the one thought also eventually goes and the mind will be extinguished at its source.

While there are many different methods for spiritual practice, according to some the most effective is Self-enquiry. For the subsistence of the mind there is no other means more effective than Self-enquiry. Even though the mind subsides by other means, that is only apparently so; it will rise again. Self-enquiry is the direct method. All other methods are practiced while retaining the ego, and therefore, many doubts arise and the ultimate question still remains to be tackled in the end. But in this method the final question is the only one and is raised from the very beginning.

Why should Self-enquiry alone be considered the direct path to Self-realization? Every kind of path except Self-enquiry presupposes the retention of the mind as the instrument for following it and cannot be followed without the mind. The ego may take different and ever more subtle forms at different stages of one's practice, but it is never destroyed. The attempt to destroy the ego or the mind by methods other than Self-enquiry is like a thief turning policeman to catch the thief that is himself.

The aim of Self-enquiry is to discover, by direct experience, that the mind is really non-existent. That is, the very existence of the mind is called into question. For most individuals, the existence of the mind, which is but a bundle of thoughts, is taken for granted as a real entity. To further complicate the problem, every conscious activity of the mind/body revolves around the tacit assumption that there is an 'I' who is doing something. It is this 'I' who makes the assumption that it is responsible for all its activities. The individual's 'I' naturally, though mistakenly, assumes "I am thinking my thoughts;" "I am performing various actions." In each and every activity the common factor is the 'I'-thought, a mental modification of the true 'I'.

Everyone in the entire world says "I", but who is making an effort to know what that "I" exactly is? One usually means by 'I', this 'body.' On a deeper level, individuals mean their faculties of thinking/feeling/willing. One can easily understand that the body is not 'I', since it is insentient and inert. The Upanishads describe it thus: "The body is built up with bones, smeared over with flesh, covered with skin, filled with *faeces*, urine, bile, phlegm, marrow, fat."[20] By this analysis, one can understand that the body is always what is known and not the knower.

A similar analysis applies to one's thoughts. If the body were you, why do you say, "My body?" If the thoughts are you, why do you say, "My thoughts?" Does anyone ever say, "I am my shirt," "I am my gold ring?" "My" is a personal possessive pronoun. These things belong to "me," the owner, the perceiver, the experiencer. So who is this "I" who possesses all these various things? One mistakes this superimposition of one's body and mind for a fact, and thereby thinks that their body and thoughts are what one refers to as "I." Further, not only does the mind perpetuate this delusion by superimposing the body and thoughts upon the Self, one's mind deceives the individual into becoming attached to sense-objects, thereby forgetting their real nature. The Self is never deluded, just as a person awake is not deluded by the dreams of the dreamer. The Self (the real 'I') never imagines that it is doing anything. The 'I' that imagines action is a doer, a thinker, a perceiver, a mental fiction, a mental modification superimposed upon the Self.

Then, what is this 'I'? In the body arises a sense of awareness.

20 *Mandukya Upanisad* 3.4.

As a collection this is usually called the mind. What is the mind but a collection of thoughts? And this collection is where the 'I' functions as their basis. Every thought relates to you, the 'I', either directly about you or connected with you as individuals, objects, things, events, presuppositions. In other words, every thought is rooted in one's 'I'. So what is this 'I'? Where is *it* rooted? Track it to its source. This process is known as an enquiry into the Self.

One should realize that no amount of thought would enable one to realize that which is beyond thought. Thus, abide in the Self as it is. What is it that prevents one from doing this? The Self ever shines, ever present. Instead of abiding in the Self, the ego, the 'I'-thought arises; the thought that I am a separate individual who believes that I am the body. This ego is the first or root thought, the first 'I'-thought. Every other thought, all second and third person pronouns (he, she, it, them) need this 'I'-thought to exist, for it is the foundation upon which they rest. To remain as the Self, all one need do is to remove this initial obstruction, the first thought, the ego, the I-am-the-body thought, or what Advaita calls 'me and mine.'

Between the ever-luminous Self (which neither rises nor sets) and the non-real, not-Self, the insentient body (which cannot of its own accord say, "I"), arises a false 'I' which is limited to the body, the ego, and this meeting place is known as the knot between the sentient Self and the insentient body. When the knot forms, ideas of bondage, desire, the entire world of multiplicity arise. When this knot is cut, liberation happens. The Upanishads say, "When all the knots that fetter here the heart are cut asunder, then a mortal becomes immortal."[21]

How does this false 'I' arise? It grasps a form/a body. By grasping, it feeds upon forms and endures. Leaving one form, it grasps another, devouring, growing, enduring. So long as one does not enquire into whom this false 'I' is, it will continue to live and thrive. The ego appears to possess consciousness and shine with the 'I'-thought and, at same time, the ego is limited to a form and it rises and sets. How clever! Like a ghost in a closet, it survives only until one, not being afraid of it any longer, enquires, opens the closet door, and finds that the ghost has vanished.

Why does ego, the 'I'-thought, disappear when enquired into? It exists only when grasping forms. Without names and forms it

---

21 *Katha Upanisad* 2.3.15.

cannot live. All thoughts, all objects, all knowledge are only name and form, whether gross or subtle. The 'I'-thought has no form of itself. To attend to itself, that is, to investigate and enquire into its source, makes it lose strength, subside, and finally disappear without a trace. There are not two 'I's, the ego and the Self. There is not duality during spiritual practices and non-duality during liberation. There is only the ocean of Consciousness, one and non-dual, the Self. It is in this ocean of Consciousness that all ideas/feelings/thoughts/names and forms arise. Are they real? No. Do they appear? Yes.

Moreover, thoughts arise because one accepts them, one lets them in. They do not impose upon us. They have no power of their own. They gain power only by our attending to them. Do not focus on them and they will subside. Whether they come or whether they go, what does it matter? To accept them, and then to struggle with them, is to give them life.

It should be noted that the mind functions only when the 'I'-thought functions. Deep sleep reveals the truth of this. All thoughts function only when the 'I'-thought is there. When the 'I'-thought is not there, the world, the mind, and the body do not exist. Anyone can observe that the mind is quiet, that it disappears, when one is deep asleep and that it only reappears upon waking. This means that the 'I'-thought daily rises and sets. Follow the 'I'-thought back to its point of rising. See where it sets. This 'I'-thought is the one necessary clue one has to discover who one really is.

For a person to eliminate the body/mind as 'not I', and so on is a beginning, and this method has often been mentioned in Advaita in order to guide a seeker to the Self. This is the time honored "not-this, not this" *(neti, neti)* technique. It is well known that the Self cannot be directly indicated. The Self is unknowable, not because it is unknown, but because it is the basis of all knowledge. It is Consciousness itself. "Words return along with the mind, not attaining it."[22] "The eye does not go there, nor speech, nor mind. The Absolute is not to be known as such and such."[23] A person who eliminates the 'not-I' cannot eliminate the 'I'. In order to be able to say, "I am not this," there must be an "I" to say it! If one uproots the ego, all else will automatically be uprooted.

---

22 *Taittirīya Upaniṣad* 2.4.1.
23 *Kena Upaniṣad* 1.3-5; *Kena Upaniṣad* 3, "It is other than all that is known, and It is also beyond the knower."

When a practitioner begins the process of Self-enquiry, it starts as a mental activity. The mind commences its enquiry into the 'I'-thought again and again, but is often distracted by other habitual thoughts that arise throughout the day. As the practice deepens and the seeker is able to hold onto its investigation into the source of the 'I'-thought, there arises a subtle subjectively experienced feeling of 'I' that persists. When this feeling ceases to connect and identify with thoughts and objects, even this feeling subsides. Then, what remains is direct experience of Being in which all sense of individuality ceases to operate.

At first, this feeling will be intermittent, but with repeated effort, it gradually becomes easier and easier to maintain. At this level, Self-enquiry has become as effortless awareness in which individual effort is no longer possible since the 'I' who makes effort has temporarily ceased to exist. This is not yet full and complete Self-realization since the 'I'-thought periodically reasserts itself. When this experience is repeated, as often as is necessary, it begins to weaken, and often destroy, the latent mental tendencies that were causing the 'I'-thought to reappear. Finally, when the latent tendencies are sufficiently weakened, the power of the Self destroys them all and, being destroyed, they will never rise again. This is complete Self-realization.

One may observe how practical and easy the technique of Self-enquiry is. There is no struggling with the mind. There is no suppression of thoughts. All it requires is for the seeker to keep an awareness of the source from which all thought springs. Abiding in the source of the 'I'-thought is the method. Abiding in the source of the 'I'-thought is the goal. Effort in the beginning is essential, but once awareness of the 'I'-thought has been firmly established, further effort is counter-productive. As well, a remarkable feature of the path of Self-enquiry is that it can be practiced any time, anywhere, while driving the car, while eating, while at work, and so on.

Generally, a human being directs all one's thoughts, actions, everything, outwards. This is because the sense organs are turned outwards and attuned to contacting things from the outside. To turn within is the first requirement regarding the question, "Who am I?" An individual, whose attention is turned outwards, by that very act, excludes any possibility of discovering who they really are. An object, the known, will never be the knower. Yet strangely, even in the act of turning outwards, the divine consciousness within one is not excluded. It is merely unnoticed.

This Reality that exists within each and every person is pure Awareness, the Self. The name does not matter. It is what the various names are pointing towards that is of paramount importance. No person can even say that they do not know it. In the very act of denying its existence, one must presuppose it to deny it! No one can say, "I do not exist." Who is the I who is saying that they do not exist? Of nothing else in the universe, or beyond the universe, can this be said of. This is the uniqueness and specialty of this consciousness, though, until it is experienced it might as well be said to not exist at all. The Self is nearer than the nearest and yet seemingly farther than the farthest. It is only when you search for It, that you lose It. You cannot take hold of It, but then you cannot get rid of It.

All the various spiritual disciplines, such as singing devotional songs, repetition of a *mantra*, breath control, meditation, and the like, are helpful, beneficial, and purificatory aids for spiritual aspirants at a particular time. A mother prepares baby food for the baby; she asks the teenager to get his or her own meal; and she leaves it to adults to eat as they wish. What is proper and needful for one person is not necessarily proper and needful for all.

JOHN ALLEN GRIMES received his B.A. in Religious Studies from the University of California at Santa Barbara and his M.A. and Ph.D. in Indian Philosophy from the University of Madras. He has taught at universities in the United States, Canada, Singapore, and India. His books include: *The Vivekacudamani: Sankara's Crown Jewel of Discrimination; A Concise Dictionary of Indian Philosophy; Ganapati: Song of the*

Self; Problems and Perspectives in Religious Discourse: Advaita Vedanta Implications; *Sapta Vidha Anupapatti: The Seven Great Untenables*; *Quest for Certainty; The Naiskarmyasiddhi of Suresvara,* and most recently, *Ramana Maharshi: The Crown Jewel of Advaita.* He currently spends his time writing and traveling between California and Chennai.

THE INFINITE WORD

Swami Atmarupananda

"LET THERE BE LIGHT," said God in the book of Genesis, "and there was light."[24] *Y-H-V-H*, God didn't go to the workshop, mix chemicals together, and, at the end of much labor, pour out the resulting light. God's word was creative. "Let there be light," he said, and there it was.

John says in the Christian gospel, "In the beginning was the Word, and the Word was with God, and the Word was God . . . All things came into being through him, and without him not one thing came into being . . ."[25] That is, all things came into being through the Word, which was God.

This is the foundation of *mantra yoga*, the meditational use of sacred words and phrases known as mantras. As the *Rig Veda* says: "The Creator existed before all this. His second was the Word. Word is indeed the supreme Brahman"—phrase for phrase, the same as the words of John.[26] Not that John plagiarized the *Rig Veda*, for such truths come from direct, mystical experience, and it is in search of such experience that mantras are in turn used.

One might wonder, how could the Word be the Infinite, which the *Upanishads* declare to be beyond mind and speech? Yes, infinite Reality is beyond words, yet it is the intent of Word, the inner meaning of Word, that which Word expresses. The Sanskrit grammarians said that the primary import of *every* word is God.

So what is a *mantra?* The traditional derivation of the Sanskrit word is *mananaat traayate iti mantra*, which means, "A *mantra* is that by thinking of which one is taken across the ocean of transmigratory existence." A *mantra*, thus, is a tool of transcendence.

---

24 Genesis 1:3 (NRSV).
25 John 1:1-3 (NRSV).
26 *Rig-Veda* 12:5.

Where do mantras come from? It is claimed that they are heard in states of deep unitive consciousness known as *samadhi*. The *mantra* we repeat and write is the closest approximation to those supersensuous sounds possible in human speech. A *mantra* as heard in deep contemplation is made of pure consciousness. It is a manifestation of pure consciousness *and is a manifestor* of pure consciousness. That is, it is revealed in a high state of consciousness, and it has the power to reveal that state of consciousness. A *mantra* is a very subtle sound, far above the physical vibrations of audible speech, far above the mental vibrations of mental chatter, and yet approximated in physical and mental sound.

"Far above the physical vibrations of audible speech." That indicates that there are levels of Word, and indeed, the science of *mantra* is based on this experiential truth. These levels are elaborated not only in the Hindu tradition, but also by the great Sufi mystic Al-Ghazzali as well:

> Let the seeker . . . sit alone in some corner, let him see to it that nothing save God—the Most High—enters his mind. Then, as he sits alone in solitude, let him not cease saying continuously with his tongue "Allah, Allah," keeping his thought on it. At last he will reach a state where the motion of his tongue will cease, and it will seem as though the word flowed from it. Let him persevere in this, until all trace of motion is removed from his tongue and he finds his heart persevering in the thought. Let him still persevere until the form of the word—its letters and shape—is removed from his heart, and there remains the idea alone, as though clinging to his heart, inseparable from it. Nothing now remains but to await what God will open to him. If he follows the above course, he may be sure that the light of the Real will shine in his heart.[27]

Here Al-Ghazzali speaks of the four levels of Word described in the Hindu tradition. There is the spoken, audible word: ". . . let him not cease saying continuously with his tongue . . ." Then the seeker is to continue until "all trace of motion is removed from his tongue." This is the mental level of speech. From the mental level one rises to the intuitive level, where "the form of the word—its letters and shape—is removed from his heart, and there remains

27 Quoted in Swami Yatiswarananda, *Meditation and Spiritual Life,* 407.

the idea alone." From there, the Word Absolute, God as Word, is revealed, and "the light of the Real will shine in his heart."

Mantra yoga is based on the experience of countless sages like Al-Ghazzali who found that the Word, especially sacred words called mantras, can lead us from physical sound to the Light of God.

Are all mantras Sanskrit? Hindu and Buddhist mantras, yes, but names like *Allah* and Jesus are revealed names as well. Mary didn't name her son after a favorite uncle. The angel Gabriel told her, "You . . . shall call his name Jesus."[28]

But one could object, 'Jesus' is an English corruption of the original name, and so how could it be considered revealed? Yes, it is the English form of the word, but there is a linguistic logic to the change of sounds from one language to another, and so the name Jesus also will take us to the Reality that Jesus is. To speak more colloquially and less philosophically—but none the less truly—does even a human mother reject her child's plea of "Ma, Ma"? Does she say, "I'll come to you when you can say 'Mother' properly!" Isn't the Divine greater, wiser, and more loving than an ordinary mother? We're not talking about a mechanical process, even though we are speaking from the standpoint of philosophical principles. We're speaking of the loving heart of Divine Wisdom.

How does one get a *mantra?* Traditionally, from a teacher. Yes, one can find mantras in books, and it does no harm to repeat a *mantra* learned from a book. But it is consciousness that enkindles consciousness, just as the flame of one candle lights other candles: it isn't the candle, but the flame of the candle that lights other candles. This, at least, is the traditional belief: a *mantra* transmitted by a qualified teacher is awakened by the teacher's consciousness.

With all of this background, we come to actual practice. The background, however, is important. One of the central problems in *mantra* practice is that it becomes unconscious. Having a context of understanding for the practice helps overcome unconscious repetition.

The practice of a *mantra* is called *japa,* that is, the rhythmical repetition of a *mantra,* aloud or mentally. Rhythmical? Yes, because the universe it made up of nothing but rhythmical patterns,

---

28 Luke 1:31 (NRSV).

and rhythm affects the mind and body deeply. How many times should we repeat it? The more the better; though of course one has to build capacity and not do too much in the beginning. It's like any exercise. Weightlifting, for instance: if we aren't straining, we aren't exercising. But there is a point where the strain is too much, and we realize that we might pop something. With a little experience we learn the distinction between healthy strain and danger.

Which is better, vocalized repetition or silent, mental repetition? Mental is better, if one can keep one's attention focused. However, most find that in the beginning it helps at least to form the *mantra* with the mouth, even if left unvocalized, or to say it softly. It should be remembered that a *mantra* given by a *guru* in the Hindu tradition should never be uttered within the hearing of another, nor should it ever be told to anyone, not because it is secret but because it is too sacred to be externalized, socialized, objectified, whereby it loses its power. This of course doesn't apply to mantras used in congregational chanting like *'Om,' 'Om namah Shivaya,'* and *'Ram,'* of the Hindu tradition, *'Om mani padme hum'* or *'Gate gate paragate parasamgate bodhi svaha'* of the Buddhist tradition, or *'Allah,' 'Jesus,'* and other such 'public' sacred words of other traditions.

What about speed of repetition? I once asked an adept at *japa*, a monk who had practiced it for over sixty years, whether fast repetition or slow repetition was better. He said that everyone has their own natural rhythm. Until that reveals itself, it is best to do it according to one's taste. But, he added, never repeat it so fast that its pronunciation is unclear.

When should it be repeated? Traditionally the hours before dawn and at sunset are said to be the best, but that's next to impossible for present-day people: modern society follows mechanical clock-time, not natural rhythms. Therefore, for most it is best to have a fixed time, as far as possible, for formal practice twice a day, in the morning and in the evening. If twice a day is impossible, then once a day. For how long? It is far better to do it for twenty minutes every day than to do it for three hours several days in a row and then not again for a month. Let us pick an amount of time as our base time that we can devote every day. Beyond that, we should do it as often as possible.

In our tradition we speak about "good *japa* work," meaning tasks that don't require too much mental engagement, allowing us to practice mental repetition as we work: sweeping, dishwashing, carpentry, driving, lawn mowing, are all examples of good *japa* work. Then, it is good to make a habit of repeating our *mantra* during quiet moments of relaxation at work or at home or in recreation. We shouldn't *work* at it at such times, but let the gentle rhythm soothe our nerves, calm our mind, and bathe our being in God's presence.

How should we repeat the *mantra*, or with what attitude should we repeat it? It can be repeated as we try to absorb ourselves in its meaning, which is God, or the impersonal Reality if we follow the path of knowledge. That is, the *meaning* of a genuine *mantra* is God, not a concept of God but the reality of God. It can be repeated as a prayer, where each repetition is an expression of our existential need for guidance, for protection, for love, for nurture, for revelation. It can be an act of worship: we lay ourselves with each repetition on the altar of love. It can be an act of Self-inquiry: from where does Word arise within me? It can be mental *karma yoga:* I mentally repeat it over all beings and even over material creation, calling out the Divine which exists within all, and blessing all with their real name, which is God's name. It can be self-purification and protection: as I repeat it I imagine it rising from the heart as a sacred fountain of sound, breaking over my head and bathing my entire being in its sacred vibration.

Vibration: that's an important point to remember. Sound is vibration. But everything is vibration, that is, rhythmical patterns in different media. And so as we repeat the *mantra*, it is helpful to think that our entire being—physical and mental—begins to vibrate in harmony with the *mantra*.

Another help in the practice: eventually, the *mantra* awakens, becomes conscious, and repeats itself. Imagination helps in that process. Thus, though we are repeating the *mantra* by an act of will in the beginning, we should imagine that the mantra repeats itself, rising from the spiritual heart in the lower center of the chest.

A disciple of Sri Ramakrishna used to say that we should salute the *mantra* at the beginning of each practice in order to reinforce the idea that it is conscious, the embodiment of Divinity. We don't salute walls, we salute conscious beings.

But doesn't the practice become mechanical? Yes, inevitably in the early years. Therefore we need to keep trying to inject awareness into the process, and that is what meditation practice is all about. One of the wonderful aspects of *japa* is this: even when mechanical it tends to continue, and as it continues it keeps breaking into our awareness and reminding us of what we are supposed to be doing. As Sri Sarada Devi, a great saint of India, used to say, it doesn't matter whether you jump into the water or are pushed into the water, you are going to get wet. Even if you say the *mantra* without concentration, it will help. Eventually, however, it has to become fully conscious.

Finally, as we repeat the *mantra* during formal meditation and again whenever we can remember it during the day and night, we find that a point comes where it is our default mental occupation: whenever the mind becomes quiet, *japa* begins. Even then it will only be half conscious, but that's a very good sign. It shows that the unconscious mind has accepted the *mantra*, and the *mantra's* own power will be working. Then all we need to do is to inject more and more awareness into the process, and one day the *mantra* will awaken and begin to repeat itself, transforming our minds and bodies, carrying us back toward the Divine Mother, revealing the light of the Real.

SWAMI ATMARUPANANDA was born in Spartanburg, South Carolina and joined the Ramakrishna Order in 1969, spending five years training at the Vivekananda Monastery in Ganges, Michigan. In 1975, he entered the monastic training college of the Ramakrishna Order of Monks in Calcutta, India. From 1977 through 1981 he spent five years at Mayavati, the remote Advaita Ashrama in the Himalayas, working as the assistant editor for the English monthly *Prabuddha Bharata* (Awakened India). In 1979, he took *sannyasa* from his *guru,* receiving his present name. Returning to the U.S. in 1982, he settled at the Ramakrishna Monastery in Trabuco Canyon, California. In 1984 he was posted to the San Diego branch of the Vedanta Society of Southern California, becoming its resident minister in 1987. In September 1997, he moved to Stone Ridge, New York, to found the Vivekananda Retreat,

Ridgely, where he served as the resident minister until 2005. Today, he is once again living at the Ramakrishna Monastery in Trabuco Canyon. He is a member of the Snowmass Interreligious Conference and a frequent teacher for the Spiritual Paths Foundation.

Indigenous Practices

ENTERING THE FLOWER WORLD:
A MEXICAN PATH TO THE SOUL

Grace Alvarez Sesma

WHEN ONE THINKS OF meditation practices and mystical thought, sadly the philosophical tradition of Mesoamerican peoples does not immediately come to most people's mind. Yet in today's Mexico, the rich spiritual heritage of the Aztec, Maya, and other tribes is preserved through a syncretic healing tradition called Curanderismo. Here the soul, mind, body, community, and environment are inseparable from Spirit and healing.

Meditation and prayer, flowers and songs, the sound of conch and whistle, aromatic oils and herbs, precious stones and river rocks, sacred feathers of eagle and hummingbird, beeswax candles patted and shaped by an elder; patients tenderly wrapped within the folds of a curandera's *rebozo*, or 'shawl,' that has been woven by hand with reverential exactitude to honor the days of the old calendar, and the Four Winds, symbolizing the directions. These are all part of the beautiful tapestry of Curanderismo, also known as Traditional Mexican Medicine.

Within the navel of the Earth, the center of the Universe, the four directions, we pray, grounded lovingly on our holy Mother Earth in order to transcend the seductiveness of polarities. We acknowledge Ometecuhtli and Omecihuatl, the Lord and Lady of Duality, the earthly manifestations of divine male and female energy; of stillness and movement, hot and cold, night and day, heaven and earth, that we may enter into oneness with Ometeotl. The peoples of Mesoamerica had many names for this aspect of ultimate unity: Kukulcan, Tepeu, Gucumatz, Chamahua, Quetzalcoatl.

The words of the Huehues, the 'Old Ones,' reflect the desire of seekers from pre-contact times to today to merge with Chamahua. This is beautifully evident in the ancient song, Icnocuicatl, 'Songs of Reflection':

Who am I? As a bird I fly about, I sing of flowers; I compose songs, butterflies of song. Let them burst forth from my soul! Let my heart be delighted with them! Our priests, I ask of you: From whence come the flowers that enrapture man? The songs that intoxicate, the lovely songs? Only from His home do they come, from the innermost part of heaven, only from there comes the myriad of flowers . . .[29]

Ancestral wisdom has been handed down century after century from elder to student guiding us to consciously cultivate spiritual practices that will help us enter *El Gran Silencio,* 'the Great Silence.' By communing with our greatest teacher, Nature, we are blessed by water, fire, earth, and air; flowers, plants, trees, and animal relations generously share their knowledge with us. Fasting for days in hidden caves and on sacred mountains, we gather *chu'lel,* 'energy' from the universe, which emanates from the All, not only for ourselves, but to help us as we offer ourselves in service to our communities.

It is *chu'lel,* the life-force that emanates from the Omnipresent that the curandero or curandera (male or female curer) accesses to help restore a patient's well-being.

Respected Yoeme/Lacandon Maya elder, Cachora Matorral affirms these truths when he says: "Spirituality is meditation. It is from this focus of the spirit that all health comes. There is only one Great Spirit. It is the soul, the one who heals, the Great Spirit, the divine. It is Chamahua. I merge with Chamahua so he can help me to help the ill person."

The practitioner of Traditional Mexican Medicine is not only a healer of the body, but also a restorer of faith in one's own inner wisdom, and in something larger and more sublime than oneself. The curandera guides us in non-judgmental, fearless self-reflection. By sharing both happy and painful personal experiences, she gives us both a reality-check and inspiration to follow our dreams. In many instances she is a spiritual midwife, helping us give birth to new paths and new ideals. She helps us recognize the unconscious creation of obstacles to a life lived with sacred purpose, whether as homemaker, student, teacher, or doctor. With aromatic bundles of plants and flowers she shifts the energy of painful personal histories to uncover the beauty of our inner sun, our inner light.

29 Leon-Portilla, Miguel, ed., *Native Mesoamerican Spirituality,* 204.

Aspiring to live with wholeness and holiness we begin to embody in our day-to-day life the Aztec spiritual principle of *Nehua ti Nehua,* "I am you, you are me." With this principle as our guide, we are inspired to see our own flaws, as well as each other's, with compassion and forgiveness—as well as with an increased feeling of kinship and ecological respect for our Mother Earth and for all beings who live in and on her. We are free to celebrate our triumphs with equanimity, and free to share the unique gifts that we bring to our relationships and to our global community.

SUNRISE, SUNSET MEDITATION

Although this meditation is best done outdoors, where you can more easily connect with the forces of nature, it can also be done in the privacy of your own backyard. Begin by standing (later you will sit). If you have a disability, the entire meditation may be performed while sitting in a chair.

1. Purifying with Sacred Herbs

Indigenous people around the world have for centuries traditionally burned ceremonially harvested herbs to purify themselves before praying, consecrating a space, or participating in ceremony. In Mexico, and in some South American traditions, a pungent resin, copal, which is secreted by pine trees, is used. Along with its many utilitarian applications—for example, making glue and crafts—traditional healers employ copal for its curative properties. Copal comes in various colors, the most easily found is a golden rich amber, the fragrance which is known to assist in entering altered states of consciousness, for removing unwanted energies, and for spiritual protection. In the United States, metaphysical shops and herb shops (as well as their Hispanic equivalent, botanicas) often carry copal.

A small fireproof earthen bowl is used in which we place and light a charcoal tablet. Sprinkle a few grains of the copal on the charcoal until it begins to release a light smoke. Bring the smoke towards your head, eyes, mouth, and heart. The intention is to cleanse our thoughts, our sight, our speech, and our emotions of negativity and doubt. We offer a prayer to the Four Winds for guidance and protection, for ourselves and for all our relations. As the fragrant smoke fills our senses, our awareness shifts and we are ready to begin our meditation.

2. Greeting Grandfather Sun

While standing quietly, face the sunrise/sunset. Breathe gently and deeply. Bring your arms up, raising them to form a triangle with your hands a few inches above the center of your head (index finger to index finger, thumb to thumb to form the triangle in the space between your hands). Palms should be facing out, towards the sun. Feel the light of Grandfather Sun enter the center of the triangle that is formed by the palms of your hands and into the space two to three inches above the top of your head. Your hands will begin to feel warm and somewhat heavy. Mentally or out loud, gratefully acknowledge the dawn of the new day (or the sunset of the day now ending). With deep thankfulness allow the blessings that Grandfather Sun brings to you and to all beings on Mother Earth to permeate your body. From above your head to below your feet, the golden light of Grandfather Sun clears your mind of misperceptions and confusion. Warm vitality, clarity and awareness flows throughout your body-mind.

After a few minutes, slowly lower your arms, keeping your hands in a triangle, until they reach your heart area. Feel the warmth of the sunlight enter your heart, cleansing it of any fear. Your heart opens, and a feeling of deep compassion and love for oneself and all of creation is felt throughout our body-mind.

After a few minutes, slowly lower your arms, keeping your hands in the shape of a triangle until you reach your stomach area. Feel the warmth of the sunlight release any tension you may be holding here. You feel clear, relaxed, and grounded. Slowly lower your arms to your sides.

3. Sitting on Mother Earth

Lower yourself to the Earth until you are seated. Feel her softness, strength, and support. Take four deep breaths. Place one hand lightly on each knee. Your shoulders and elbows are relaxed. Keeping your eyes open, focus on one object in your immediate vicinity. If it moves, track it with your eyes. Do your best not to blink for as long as you are able. Allow your eyes to tear up; this is part of the cleansing which is produced by this part of the meditation.

After at least three to five minutes, allow your eyes to close. For the next 20 minutes, focus on your breathing. It should be gentle, normal breathing, filling your abdomen and lungs effortlessly. Maintaining attention on your heart, feel your connection to *ehecatl,* 'Wind,' as it caresses you softly. Nature, trees, plants, and birds share their sacred breath with you. Our holy Mother Earth shares her energy with you, and you gratefully allow it to enter your body, to heal and support you. You relax in the awareness that you are a part of *chu'lel.* Take four deep breaths and return to everyday awareness.

Consciously linking to all that is around us through meditation feeds our soul, nurtures our hearts, heals our bodies and deepens our connection to all our relations. Our spiritual practice begins to have a subtle but powerful influence in our life, personally and professionally. It helps heal and bring the gently empowering effect of love and peace upon our families, our communities and our world. May all spiritual paths join in the spirit of love, to bring peace to you, to us, to all those who come after. Ometeotl.

GRACE ALVAREZ SESMA is Mexican of Kumeyaay/Yoeme/ Mexica heritage, born in Baja California, Mexico. She has studied traditional healing with several indigenous healers from Mexico as well as the United States, principally with noted elder, Yoeme/Lacandon Maya, Cachora Matorral of Mexico. She is Adjunct Professor at Arizona Western College in Yuma, Arizona where she teaches "Exploring Native American Medicine Ways: Learning from, and honoring, Indigenous Healing Traditions." Grace has a consulting and private healing practice, which draws from Aztec and Mayan spiritual and healing traditions. She collaborates with physicians to integrate western allopathic medicine with traditional Mesoamerican healing and lectures nationally on *curanderismo*. A leader in the Latina community, in 1993 she was the recipient of the prestigious leadership fellowship award by the National Hispana Leadership Institute in collaboration with Harvard University's John F. Kennedy School of Government.

THE INIPI CEREMONY
& CRYING FOR A VISION

Four Arrows

THE INIPI CEREMONY

> *I am going to venture that the man who sat on the ground*
> *in his* tipi *meditating on life and its meaning, accepting*
> *the kinship of all creatures, and acknowledging unity with*
> *the universe of things, was infusing into his being the true*
> *essence of civilization.*
>
> — Luther Standing Bear

AMONG AMERICAN INDIAN contemplative rituals, perhaps the most generally well-known is what people often speak of as the 'sweat lodge.' Although American Indians and non-Indians alike use this English term today, the appropriation and use of the sweat lodge ceremony by non-Indians is often looked upon in traditional circles as representing a desecration of Native spiritual traditions. The most extreme example of such a desecration is what happened in 2009 when three individuals who had paid large sums of money to participate in a sweat lodge died and 18 others were hospitalized while supposedly under the care of James Ray and his multi-million dollar spirituality business.[30]

Although sweat lodges are used in various Indigenous cultures throughout North and South America, I will refer to the Lakota versions in this essay. Their words for the practice are *inipi* and *oinikaga*. The first refers to making life anew. The second more pointedly describes a 'house of purification.' Both are a way of life

---

30 For this negligent misappropriation of their ritual, the Lakota Nation is currently suing many involved, including the state of Arizona where the business was allowed to operate.

rather than a religious event per se, but whatever it is called, the *inipi* is not taken lightly, and no one is allowed to lead an *inipi* without having served a minimum of four years of apprenticeship.

Now, the reader of this book might be wondering, "If one must serve an apprenticeship to lead an *inipi*, and if First Nations' Peoples are deeply concerned about non-Indians 'appropriating' their spiritual traditions, what can Four Arrows say in a short aritcle about using the *inipi* as a contemplative resource here?" Well, I actually considered the option of simply creating a bibliography of selected publications on this subject. However, such a 'cop out' would not likely have been acceptable to the editor, So, instead I have chosen to speak from my heart in a way that will hopefully serve the highest good. I will try my best to—honor traditional Lakota beliefs; avoid the 'wannabe' rationales that can lead to exploitation; avoid the crime of minimizing complicated, sacred ceremonial customs; and invoke a sense of reciprocity among those who enter this arena with pure intentions and mindful actions. In so doing, I hope to offer the interested reader something that will truly help introduce American Indian spirituality in a positive and meaningful way, the 'Indian way.'

Of course, I understand the risks of my potential failure, but I also believe that the desperate imbalance of our world today warrants the effort. In 1993, a "Declaration of War Against Exploiters of Lakota Spirituality" was passed at a gathering of 500 representatives from 40 tribes.[31] As with many issues in Indian country, people are divided on this proclamation. To illustrate this split with a personal story, I once I sang a sacred Lakota 'thank-you song' at a gathering of Navajo and non-Indian parents at a school in Arizona. Within moments, one Navajo medicine man came up and told me I should know better than to take such a song out of the *inipi*. Within a few more minutes, another equally respected spiritual leader came up and thanked me for "taking the song outside the circle."

The reasons for the proclaimation are understandable and largely valid. However, if the Lakota prayer, *Mitakuye Oyasin* ('we are all related') is interpreted correctly, how can one culture's traditions be so exclusive? Where is the balance-point that takes the two truths out of the duality they now suffer? Here is my humble offering as to how we might achieve this:

---

31 The document can easily be found on-line.

1. Avoid any association with commercialization or consumerism that may be connected to the *inipi*. If money is a requirement for praying for or meditating on increasing health and harmony, individually or collectively, move on. After all, the consumerism of our times has contributed in many ways to the loss of balance that the *inipi* intends to restore.

2. With this first 'rule' in mind, it is nonetheless vital to 'give back' something to the People whose traditional ways you are employing. There are multiple avenues for such reciprocity.

3. Find someone who speaks the language and has led purification lodges for many years so you can learn if this is a tradition with which your spirit resonates.

4. Learn everything you can within reason about the sacred symbolism and local etiquette related to the specific customs and practices. Then, have the humility to realize that you still know very little.

5. If you cannot find a qualified *inipi* leader and you wish to build your own lodge and 'pour the water' yourself, use the information from your research to build a proper lodge according to whatever traditional cultural model you choose.

6. Once the lodge is constructed, learn what 'grandfathers' (rocks) are safe to use and how to properly heat them. Then, do at least four lodges solo before inviting friends to share with the experience with you.

7. Make a studious and intuitive decision about whether your lodge will be co-ed or not. Some Lakota traditionalists are against women participating because of ideas relating to purpose. They see the *inipi* as an opportunity for purification, regeneration and gaining intuitive knowledge. These are all things a woman already can do according to traditional views, whereas men must work at accomplishing them via the *inipi*. On the other hand, times and abilities have changed and it may be that both sexes are in need of the extra effort now.

8. If you choose to run a not for profit purification lodge for friends, spend time before entering the lodge to explain your

pitiful lack of qualifications, expressing much humility. Give your particular guidelines, being sure to tell people that if it gets too hot for someone, he or she should take a moment to endure just long enough to pray harder, and then if still too uncomfortable, to ask to open the door immediately by saying *"Mitakuye Oyasin"* or "We are all related," or "Open the damn door fast!"

9. Interject a sincere balance of humor if you want to come close to the authentic ways American Indians practice this ceremony. Humor can bring equity, comfort and oneness to all participants and has been used accordingly throughout Indigenous Peoples' histories. Usually the humor is reserved for the time in between the four rounds while the fresh air is circulating.

10. In addition to the humor so typically a part of purification lodge ceremonies, maintain an attitude in the lodge that assures all will know that the experience is not a game of 'playing Indian.' Lead in such a way as to reveal that truth, focus, responsibility, reciprocity, trust and peacefulness *(wolokokiciapi)* are vitally important. There can be no doubt that you are entering a sacred place where spirits may be in attendance.

11. Never allow anyone to enter the lodge if he or she consumed alcohol within 24 hours, and encourage participants to have not eaten within at least four hours before.

12. Although you will likely not learn an original language associated with the particular culture you are borrowing from when talking in the lodge, honor the spirits by learning the songs typically sung in the original language.

13. Choose the focus for each of your four rounds. There are a number of options. For example, in my lodge, we use the first round to pray for ourselves; the second to pray for whatever relations are in need (from family to creatures in the ocean); the third to restore the power of women in our world, and the last to offer appreciation for all the beauty in our lives. During each round, I ask people to pray in unison out loud while the drum is played and songs are sung to afford some privacy, but there are options, such as each person taking a turn.

Although there are many possibilities for bringing 'baggage' into the lodge that may continue the colonization of Indian Peoples, one piece I wish to mention relates to bringing in a religious orthodoxy that assumes an anthropocentric oriented deity. In the traditional *inipi*, there is, in my opinion, little room for the exclusive assumption that sees humans as superior to other sentient beings or that a 'one human-like God' worldview is a given. Although many full-blood Lakota themselves now combine the *inipi* with their acquired Christian faith and beliefs, I contend that these two assumptions do not align well with what it means to participate in an *inipi,* regardless of one's heritage. Individuals can have such beliefs, but must somehow leave them outside the *inipi* if they are to honor it. Humans cannot be considered to be above other beings, whether grasses, ants, or what have you in a traditional Lakota ceremony. The concept of *Wakan Tanka* is not perceived as a singular human-oriented figure, but rather as a 'great incomprehensible and mysterious' collection of many sacred beings gathered into one all-inclusive force.

These suggestions of mine are no doubt incomplete, and some of my Indigenous brothers and sisters will likely disagree. However, as I have said, I believe that no culture has exclusive rights to any contemplative exercise that can bring health and balance to individuals, communities, or our world at large. There is no question that we must respect the complex uniqueness of diverse ways of knowing, and do what is possible to acknowledge and sustain Indigenous People's language and cultures. At the same time, we must also realize we are all in the same boat and it is sinking. Many non-Indians feel spiritually in-tune with ancient Indigenous ways of being, and many so-called 'outsiders' have already contributed to bringing back tribal traditions that were all but lost.[32]

Regardless of our spiritual tradition, it is past time to make our every act responsible for assuring that every living thing in a particular place will survive into the future. For the many of us who have been 'misplaced' and now claim new territories, this requires that we do our best to learn about our new environment. This could well mean learning to contemplate and send out vibrations

---

32 For example, the Lakota flute, outlawed by the U.S. government was essentially reintroduced to the People by an Anglo physician.

according to the ancient *inipi* traditions associated with where our spirits now dwell.

CRYING FOR A VISION

Crying, I saw a red-breasted wood-pecker standing on the offering pole. I believe he may have given to me something of his wochangi *(power)...*
— Nicholas Black Elk

ALTHOUGH VISION QUESTS of one form or another have been used to gain new insights by people in many spiritual traditions, they are often aligned with Indigenous Peoples, especially those of North and South America. The Lakota refer to this sacred ritual as *hanblecheyapi,* which translates to 'crying for a vision.' This phrase embodies ideas that may be helpful in understanding the American Indian vision quest as a potential opportunity for the personal transformation of all individuals.

In offering these words for "all individuals," I wish to caution the non-Indian reader about using the Lakota vision quest per se, or a similar one from another Indigenous culture, without a more comprehensive experiential base. Many individuals have appropriated Indigenous sacred ceremonies, some even charging money to participate in them, without such experience and without adequate reciprocity. I think this contributes to the loss of the original culture, but is also likely to result in a diminished outcome, no matter how good the intentions. I will not attempt to describe the requirements for such a base, but offer that it includes significant degrees of respect, humility, and truth-seeking.

I also want to briefly explain my willingness to share what I know about this event and how the reader might go about utilizing it. I learned and utilized the vision quest during my years of Sun Dancing with the Oglala on Pine Ridge Indian Reservation, where I lived and worked. I am not Oglala by blood but by the name-giving ceremony. My mother possessed Cherokee blood but I was raised in stereotypical western society. In studying Indigenous Worldviews as a cognate area for my second doctoral degree, I have studied a number of other First Nations. At this point in my life,[33] I am quite convinced that the wisdom of our ancestors, the few who still retain it, rests mostly in pockets of Indigenous Peoples. I'm not referring to wisdom that might be captured in books. Rather, to a way of being in the world at all times that is in balance with the seen and unseen energies (in a world where "God has moved indoors," as my old friend, Sam Keen, once phrased it). I think it is vital for us to remember this wisdom in our imbalanced world, and if sharing certain aspects of the Lakota vision question will help anyone acquire this wisdom, I am all for it. In any case, I can only speak from my own experience, and do not pretend to represent the Lakota ceremonies with any authority.

The *hanbleceya,* or 'cry for a vision' ceremony does not describe physically sobbing, but rather refers to the need for healing or making something better or more balanced. My Cherokee ancestors refer to a vision quest as an *ut-stay-llsk,* meaning 'to help others.' Ultimately, they both say that "relationships" are essential. In Western culture, individuals often cry for their own needs. This would be rare for the traditionalists in "Indian country" whom I know. They may use a vision quest for gaining, say, personal courage, but the ultimate goal would be for helping others. For the American Indian, relationships are about giving significance to others. Thus, a vision quest is not only about helping others, but about important spiritual forces that exist in the 'other.'

Another idea behind the term, 'crying,' relates to humility. One cannot be or feel superior to any relation, nor expect favored treatment. Vision quests are about tapping into life forces of other things or beings that have power greater than ours. The Lakota call the force, *wakanda.* Visions that might come during the quest are actually spirit-helpers. They connect the person with the *wakanda* in a way that provides possibilities for a transformation.

Often the *wakanda* comes in the form of an animal. Animals, birds, fish, insects, and plants are thought of as having great power and are considered as guides for humanity. The relationship with them does not call for supplication or sacrifice, but is about gift exchange and sharing for the sake of continuing health for the community. It also reveals the animism that weaves through American Indian consciousness. *Wakan-Tanka,* the Great Mysterious, represents a vast pool of interconnections inspired with the same power, and among them are the many non-human

---

33 At the time of this writing, I am 64 years old.

guides with whom humans share life on Mother Earth.

One of my own experiences with animal spirit-helpers occurred while I was preparing for a Lakota Sun Dance *(Wiwanyag Wachipi)* while living in the Sawtooth Mountains of Idaho. The weather forecast for the event predicted 114 degree heat and I felt a rush of concern take hold of me. I wanted to pray for the world with my friends, but worried that I might not be able to concentrate optimally during the four day ordeal. Vision quests are an inherent part of preparing for the Sun Dance and I took myself, with my medicine man's instructions, to a hidden patch of trees high up the mountain. I set down the circle of tobacco ties and with only a blanket and a *chanupa* (sacred pipe), I prepared for 24 hours of crying for a vision in preparation for the Sun Dance. As soon as I sat in the circle, a rat-like creature came near my feet and I instinctively kicked it away. Immediately, I realized my ignorance. I regrouped my focus and within minutes the creature returned. It nibbled on one of the tobacco ties, then turned and faced the same direction as I as if it were a pet dog. I knew this was my 'vision,' but with 23 hours to go my Western impatience took over. What did it mean? I was far from those who might know, so my only thought was, "I have to get to a computer and learn about this rat!"

After several minutes, the rat left and I fell in and out of sleep. Unlike other *hanbleceyas* where a dream or image came instead of a creature, I remembered only this rodent. (For the Oglala, both mean a deeper awareness of *Wakan Tanka* rather than some unconscious event).

The next morning, I came down and immediately prepared the fire and *grandfathers* (stones) for the *inipi* (sweat lodge), a ritual that is also intimately connected to vision quests. Then, I ran to the computer and searched for images of North American rodents. Immediately a picture of my spirit-guide appeared. Under it was a caption that read: "Kangaroo rats, genus Dipodomys, are small rodents native to North America. They are the only mammals that do not lose water and can go a lifetime with out drinking." By the time I emerged from the second *inipi,* I had regained the confidence I needed to continue my preparations.

For those who sincerely resonate with their Indigenous ancestors or the American Indian way of knowing, I reluctantly offer the following brief instructions. I say reluctantly, because one of the first mandates is to seek assistance from someone with enough experience and knowledge to guide you, and it is unlikely most people will have such a contact. In any case, I believe it is time for all people of all faiths to at least learn about our ancient ways to live on this planet. So, I will be brief so as to encourage further assistance. Remember, this is only one way, the way I was taught:

1. If possible, gain the assistance of a qualified elder.
2. The week before, maintain healthy habits of living as best you can.
3. Make a string of tobacco ties and meditate and pray while making each. You will have to learn how to do this. It should be long enough to make a circle around you when you go to your sacred place in the wilderness.
4. Participate in an *inipi* ceremony to purify yourself.
5. Immediately after, walk or ride a horse to the hill. If possible, have the elder and/or special friends/family take you. If possible, they should retrieve you the next day. This sense of community support is important.
6. You will not likely have a *chanupa,* but go with only a blanket.
7. Whether you do one full 24 hour day or four, stay awake and sitting for as long as you can. Alternate facing each direction. Focus on your surroundings. It is OK if you sleep. There is little difference between a "waking vision" and a dream. Transformation in American Indian terms is about temporarily experiencing other realities and bringing back something useful from them.
8. Have new clothes ready for you when you return. You will put them on after your second *inipi* ceremony in which you give thanks, sing sacred songs again, and share your vision-story with others who can help you interpret them.
9. Afterwards, create something you can keep with you always that incorporates the spirit of your vision/spirit-helper. Make a medicine bundle of appropriate materials, write a poem, create a song, paint a picture and, most importantly, live according to the guidance given you.

Mitakuye Oyasin (all my relations),
Wahinkpe Topa (Four Arrows).

FOUR ARROWS (WAHINKPE TOPA), also known as Don Trent Jacobs, has doctorates in health psychology and curriculum and instruction with a specialty in Indigenous Worldviews. Of essentially Cherokee and Irish ancestry, he has fulfilled his Sun Dance vows with the Medicine Horse Oglala band. After serving as Dean of Education at Oglala Lakota College and then as a tenured associate professor at Northern Arizona University, he joined the College of Educational Leadership at Fielding Graduate University, where he mentors doctoral students and writes. He is the author of numerous books, articles, and chapters, including *Primal Awareness: A True Story of Awakening and Transformation with the Raramuri Shamans of Mexico*; *Unlearning the Language of Conquest*; *Critical Neurophilosophy and Indigenous Wisdom* (Sense), and his first novel, *Last Song of the Whales*.

Returning to Sacred Ground

Michael Kearney

Within a Celtic cosmology there are three worlds: *Cruinne, Alltar,* and *Neart*. We can visualize these as three concentric circles with *Cruinne*—the outermost circle—corresponding to space and time, the causal, material world of everyday reality. *Alltar*—the middle circle—is the realm of dreams and visions, of a-causality; it is the place we come to in deep meditation, the place we come to before we die. *Neart*—the innermost and third circle—literally means 'nothing'; it the un-manifest that is replete with all possibility. The three worlds of Celtic cosmology are not intended to represent a hierarchical value system. Each world is equally important in its own way. Within this cosmology, the 'goal' of spiritual practice is a way of being that allows us to be in all three worlds simultaneously. And when we are, we are awake, alive, and deeply connected.

Attitude

For the Celts, nature and the divine are synonymous. Nature is 'divine ground.' And nature is an embodiment of all three worlds— *Cruinne, Alltar, Neart*—as a dependently co-arising, interweaving, dynamic flux of energy and light. Think of a great tree, with the branches as *Cruinne,* the trunk as *Alltar,* and the roots as *Neart.* And imagine that each part of the tree—the branches, the trunk, and the roots—is in bloom. The whole tree is blooming.

Within a Celtic cosmology, nature is seen as 'thin place,' where the veil between worlds is porous. So when we are in nature, we are in more than one world—*nature as liminal space.* As we move into nature, we come into the 'now,' for nature is always in the present tense. The great trees standing in the morning mist never move from where they are. They are *there,* utterly there, and utterly present—*nature as embodied is-ness.*

INTENTION AND HOPE

We might consider stepping into nature as 'vision quest'; not in the sense of receiving some special vision, but of allowing nature to initiate us into another way of seeing and another way of being. Might we be open to moving from a *Cruinne*-only way of being in the world, to a *Cruinne-Alltar-Neart* way of being in the world, and to the new way of perceiving, and of behaving, that comes with this?

Irish philosopher and nature-mystic John Moriarty talks about how this can happen as a paradigm shift from "me-you consciousness" to "we-consciousness." He describes a moment where nature affected him in this way. It happened one day as he was walking on his native Kerry Mountains, very much in the grip of his demons. Suddenly, a wild hare got up from the heather at his feet and ran away. Looking down he saw the indentation of where the hare had been lying there in the heather. Letting himself down onto the ground, Moriarty lay his head in the still warm space. He lay there for some time, "Letting nature happen to him."

We each have our hopes as we head into nature. Perhaps a necessary first step is letting go of an expectation of any particular outcome. T. S. Eliot writes, "Teach us to wait without hope for hope would be hope of the wrong thing." When we first arrive in nature we are filled with our stories, our dramas, our noise; it's all about us, and what we notice and see comes from this perspective. So rather than expecting anything in particular, we might simply be aware that one possible outcome is that we will pass from being *foreground* to nature's *background,* to being background to nature's foreground.

TASKS

It begins with paying attention. Mary Oliver, whose work as a poet flows from her relationship with nature, writes: "To pay attention, this is our endless and proper work." And again, "This is the first, wildest and wisest thing I know, that the soul exists, and that it is built entirely out of attention." Paying attention is what brings us into the present moment, and into relationship. Implicit in our fully sensate attention is a quality of profound receptivity, an allowing, in Moriarty's words, "Nature happen to us." Novelist, Henry Miller, writes of the radical implications of such a letting go:

"I know what the cure is, it is to give up, to relinquish, to surrender; so that our little hearts may beat in unison with the great heart of the world."

KNOWING

How do we know if we have left the isolation of *Cruinne*-mind? How do we know if we have arrived in nature? Not in any place in particular so much as in a process, a way of seeing? How do we recognize that this has happened?

Immediately prior to this shift, there may be feelings of fear and anxiety as something in us, maybe the ego, senses that we are crossing a threshold. We are moving from a place that is familiar and domesticated, to a place that is unknown and wild. There is a kind of death involved here, a "dying before we die."

This is where we come to the limits of language and of abstract conceptualizations. This is something that the animal we are recognizes as subtle shifts in the quality of our energy and awareness. We may be aware of qualities such as lightness, and of being wide-awake; a sense of porousness, of being part of something more, of being deeply connected, of being vividly-alive.

Then, simplicity; cellular-resonance; a sense of rightness, of being in *Tao;* a sense that whatever happens, happens, and its okay, and its alright; and with it a sense of ripeness—like a plum, at the right moment, falling to the ground.

Poetry, being closer to nature, may help us to find words. William Wordsworth, "With an eye made quiet by the power of harmony, we see into the very heart of things." John Moriarty, "We have become plankton in the abyss of faith." Mark Nepo, "We are no longer gods who carve out rivers, but particles awakened in the stream." Mary Oliver, "This is how you swim inwards, this is how you flow outwards, this is how you pray." And again, "When deep in the tree all the locks click open, and the fire surges through the wood, and the blossoms blossom."

RETURNING TO SACRED GROUND MEDITATION

This meditation may be practiced in one of two ways. The first possibility is in nature itself—where you have the opportunity to wander in nature, in wilderness, knowing that there is a place waiting to be found by you, a place that is already there, a place you will simultaneously recognize and be recognized by, a place where you are already known. Finding this place comes with patience, and an open heart and mind, and is a process involving curiosity and intuition, of remembering and of being remembered.

The second possibility, which allows one to use this as a guided meditation with those who are sick or frail or confined to bed, is where we approach a remembered place in nature, with which we feel a special affinity, through the imagination.

The next paragraph is the introduction for those who are doing this meditation as an imaginal exercise:

> Begin by closing your eyes—bring your attention to the sensations of the (bed, chair, floor, or ground) supporting your body, your back, your head, your arms, pelvis, legs . . . Notice the contact between your body and the surface that supports you . . . Drop into that contact . . . aware of the gravity in the weight of your body . . . With each exhalation, let go to this gravity and to the contact and the holding support beneath you, knowing that it is there . . . Now, remember a place in nature that is special to you . . . somewhere you love to go, love to be . . . A place where you feel safe . . . A place where you feel free to be yourself—awake, alive, connected . . . Imagine yourself arriving at this place . . .

As you arrive in this place, slow down, look around; begin to take in the detail. Notice the quality of the light, the colors, any movement or other detail that catches your eye . . . Let this sink-in . . . Fully dilated, just notice, receiving whatever is there . . . You are here now! You have arrived in this place you love, this place you love to be in . . .

Now, pause. Stand still in this place . . . Notice whatever sounds there are . . . Allow them to be as they are; receive them, drink them in . . . Now bring your attention to any smell there might be in this place . . . Sniff the air . . . Is there is any characteristic aroma? You may even notice some taste in this sensation . . .

When you are ready, look around you. Locate a spot where you could easily and comfortably sit or lie. If you would like to, gently let yourself down onto the ground . . .

You are sitting or lying now, in fuller contact with the ground, with the palms of your hands face down . . . Close your eyes; bring all your awareness to the contact between your skin and the ground . . . With each exhalation, let the weight of your body drop with gravity into this contact with the ground . . . Notice the temperature, the texture, the moisture or dryness; you may even need to move your palms a little to get an even better sense of this . . . If you are sitting, notice the contact between your feet and the ground, your seat and the ground . . . If you are lying, notice the contact between your feet, your legs, your pelvis, your back, your shoulders, arms, the back of your neck, your head and the ground of this place . . .

Notice how the ground of this place is *there*—is fully and completely *there*. This ground is holding you; the ground of this place is holding you. This ground has been there all along; this ground is here, now . . .

Once again, bring your full awareness to the contact between your body and the ground. With each exhalation, let yourself go to the ground of this place. Allow yourself to deeply relax into being held in this way. Let go to this ancient gravity, this ancient ground. Let go to this place that is always there, this place that knows you more deeply than you know yourself. Let yourself go, to being held in this way, to being known in this way.

And as you relax and let go in this way, if you notice your mind being caught up in thought, gently bring your attention back to the contact between your body and the ground; and once again, and with the exhale, let go to gravity, let go to the contact with this ancient ground . . .

(You might wish to have a timer set so you can practice this meditation for 10, 15, or 20 minutes, as you choose. As your timer sounds, bring your attention back to the sounds of the place you are in; when you are ready, open your eyes.)[34]

> *Quick now, here, now, always; (a condition of complete simplicity): costing not less than everything.*
> — T.S. Eliot

---

34 I am grateful to Celtic scholar Fionntulach (www.ceilede.co.uk) for her teaching on the Celtic Three-World cosmology.

MICHAEL KEARNEY is an Irish physician with over 30 years experience in end-of-life care. He has worked in England, at St. Christopher's Hospice, in Ireland, at Our Lady's Hospice, and in Canada, at McGill Medical School. He is currently based in Santa Barbara, California, where he works as Medical Director of the Palliative Care Service at Santa Barbara Cottage Hospital and Associate Medical Director at Visiting Nurse and Hospice Care. He also acts as medical director to the Anam Cara Project for Compassionate Companionship in Life and Death in Bend, Oregon. He teaches internationally and has published two books on psycho-spiritual aspects of end-of-life care: *Mortally Wounded: Stories of Soul Pain, Death and Healing* and *A Place of Healing: Working with Suffering in Living and Dying.* He is currently working on a book about Irish nature mystic John Moriarty, and indigenous wisdom traditions.

Islamic Practices

THE ELEMENTAL
PURIFICATION BREATHS

Pir Zia Inayat-Khan

Air, earth, water and fire are God's servants. To us they seem lifeless, but to God living.[35]
— Jalal al-Din Rumi

IN THE SIXTH CENTURY C.E., the Ka'ba at Mecca was an idol house where an assortment of deities were routinely plied with fumigations and sacrifices. But not all Meccans were votaries of the cult. Some were convinced that the Ka'ba was the legacy of the prophet Abraham. These loosely organized desert monotheists were known as *hanifs*. Though lacking a bounded religious identity, the *hanifs* enjoyed a fertile inner life. One of their practices was a form of meditative retreat called *tahannuth*.

It was in the course of such a retreat, in a cave on Mount Hira, that Muhammad (d. 632) received his first revelation. Borne by the angel Gabriel, the revelation urged him, "Recite!" As the flow of divine speech resumed, Muhammad recited to those who would listen, beginning with his wife Khadija. Thus, over the space of two decades, chapter-by-chapter the *Qur'an* descended to Earth.

In places, the *Qur'an* provides fascinating glimpses into Muhammad's personal mystical experiences. The ninety-fourth chapter *(al-Inshirah,* 'The Opening Up') describes how the Prophet's breast was opened and his heart purified. Other verses speak of a "night journey" to Jerusalem, whereupon the Prophet ascended the empyrean and approached the presence of the God.[36]

Among Muhammad's followers were a cadre of disciples who sought to emulate him not merely exoterically but also esoterically,

---

35 Jalal al-Din Rumi, ed. Reynold A. Nicholson, *Masnavi-yi ma'navi,* 36.
36 Qur'an 17:1, 53:7-18.

undertaking a regimen of interior purification and uninterrupted remembrance of God (invoked in Arabic as *Allah*).[37] In time these initiates and their heirs became known as Sufis.

Early definitions of Sufism *(tasawwuf)* highlight the moral and spiritual disposition of its practitioners. The Sufi was one who "possesses nothing and is possessed by nothing," who "sees nothing but God in the two worlds," whose "thought keeps pace with his foot," and whose "language, when he speaks, is the reality of his state." For some, the very act of naming Sufism was inimical. One Sufi lamented, "Sufism was a reality without a name that has become a name without a reality."[38]

Such scruples notwithstanding, between the tenth and thirteenth centuries Sufism transformed itself into a large-scale social, intellectual and spiritual movement driven by organized mystical orders spread across the Afro-Eurasian *oikumene*, from Andalusia to Hindustan. Common to all of these groups was the project of seeking nearness with God through individual and collective spiritual practice. Within this shared framework, each order developed a method of practice more or less unique to itself.

In South Asia, the Chishti Order attained special prominence. Brought to India by Mu'in al-Din Chishti (d. 1236) and Qutb al-Din Bakhtiyar Kaki (d. 1235), it rapidly grew in influence under their successors, Farid al-Din Ganj-i Shakar (d. 1265), Nizam al-Din Awliya' (d. 1325), and Nasir al-Din Chiragh (d. 1351). All of these adepts taught silent, heart-centered contemplation *(muraqaba)* as a core practice. Nizam al-Din Awliya' attributed his method of contemplation to Abu Bakr al-Shibli (d. 945), who learned it by watching a cat poised motionless before a mouse hole.[39]

In the Mughal era, Shah Kalim Allah Jahanabadi (d. 1729)

---

37 A later Sufi, Najm al-Din Kubra (d. 1221), explained the remembrance of Allah thus: "The 'h' in the divine name 'Allah' is the very sound we make with every breath. The other letters (in the Arabic spelling: *alif* and reduplicated *lam*) represent an intensified definite article (serving to emphasize the uniqueness of Allah). The essential part of the divine name is therefore that 'h', which automatically accompanies our every breath. All life depends on the constant utterance of that noble name. As for the seeker of intimate knowledge, it is incumbent on him to recognize this subtle fact, and to maintain, with every breath, the consciousness of being with Allah." Mawlana 'Ali ibn Husain Safi, *Rashahat 'Ain al-Hayat: Beads of Dew from the Source of Life,* 18.

38 'Ali B. Thman Al-Jullabi A Hujwiri, trans. Reynold A. Nicholson, *Kashf al-Mahjub of Al Hujwiri: The Oldest Persian Treatise on Sufism,* 30-44.

39 Amir Khwurd Kirmani, *Siyar al-awlia',* 448.

compiled a systematic exposition of the major practices of the Chishti Order entitled *Kashkul-i Kalimi*. Shah Kalim Allah positions contemplation as the first stage in a three-fold process. At the stage of contemplation the seeker looks with closed eyes into the heart and visualizes God's presence within it. Later, at the stage of meditation *(mushahada),* the seeker looks toward the sky and imagines leaving the body and approaching God through the celestial spheres. Finally, at the stage of beholding *(mu'ayana),* the seeker's heart is permanently anchored in the seventh heaven by means of a golden thread.[40]

In the early twentieth century, the Chishti-Nizami-Kalimi branch of the Sufi tree flowered in the life and teachings of Inayat Khan (d. 1927). Enjoined by his teacher to bring Sufism to the West, Inayat Khan traveled extensively in the United States and Europe and in 1917 officially established his Sufi Order in London. Building on the work of his Chishti predecessors, he developed a curriculum of esoteric study emphasizing four phases of spiritual practice: concentration, contemplation, meditation, and realization. Moving through these grades, the practitioner progressively learns to focus attention, refine thought, transcend thought in pure luminous awareness, and ultimately to integrate transcendent and immanent modes of cognition.

The roots of Inayat Khan's methodology were not only Islamic, but also Indic. His transmission connected, as he phrased it, "two lines of the prophetic mission, the Hindu line and that of Beni Israel."[41] The Mughal crown prince Dara Shikuh characterized the encounter between the wisdom of the *Qur'an* and that of the *Upanishads* as a "merging of two oceans."[42] More than any other order, the Chishtis actively fostered this cultural and spiritual exchange.

Sufism and Yoga are distinctly different systems of knowledge and practice. They are united, however, by their mutual possession of an elementalist cosmology.[43] In both traditions, the elements are reverenced as primal sacred forces. For the Sufis, the elements are four in number: earth, water, fire and air. In addition to these the Vedic worldview posits a fifth element or *quintessence*: ether

---

40 Shah Kalim Allah Jahanabadi, *Kashkul-i Kalimi,* 31.
41 Inayat Khan, *The Unity of Religious Ideals,* 159.
42 Muhammad Dara Shikuh, ed. and trans. M. Mahfuz-ul-Ha, *Majma'-ul-bahrain.*
43 *The Oxford English Dictionary* defines elementalism as "a method or theory which divinizes the elemental powers of nature."

(akash).

Sufism and Yoga concur that, at the level of latent perfection, the human being is a microcosm of the universe *('alam saghir)*, physically, psychologically and spiritually endowed with the pure qualities of the four elements. For this potential to be actualized, the human form must be realigned with its cosmic matrix, the animate Earth. To accomplish this, Sufis and Yogis practice a shared repertory of exercises that function to harmonize the elements within and without.

The practice that follows is a notable exercise of this kind. Transmitted by Inayat Khan, it serves as a foundational practice within the Order he founded. While most of the esoteric disciplines taught in the Order are reserved for initiates, this simple yet profound practice is an open one. Ideally it is to be done early in the morning, outside or before an open window.

THE PRACTICE

Sit or stand in silence, erect but relaxed. Close your eyes:

Earth

Inhale and exhale through the nose five times. Stimulate the horizontal motion of the subtle energetic current of the breath. Attune to the color yellow. Identify with stone, sand, loam, and clay. Feel the bone, gristle, flesh and skin of which your body is made. Sense the chthonic dimension of your psyche, the qualities of stability, patience and humility.

Water

Inhale through the nose and exhale through the mouth five times. Stimulate the descending motion of the subtle energetic current of the breath. Attune to the color green. Identify with waves, whirlpools, torrents and rivulets. Feel the blood and lymph flowing within you, answering the beat of your heart. Sense the aqueous dimension of your psyche, the qualities of purity, compassion and generosity.

Fire

Inhale through the mouth and exhale through the nose five times. Stimulate the ascending motion of the subtle energetic current of the breath. Attune to the color red. Identify with lava, flame, sparks, and light. Feel the metabolic heat radiating from your body. Sense the igneous dimension of your psyche, the qualities of ardor and burning conviction.

Air

Inhale through the mouth and exhale through the mouth five times. Stimulate the chaotic, zigzag motion of the subtle energetic current of the breath. Attune to the color blue. Identify with the sky, the breeze, clouds, and bubbles. Feel the oxygen whirling in the airways of your body. Sense the aerial dimension of your psyche, the qualities of buoyancy, freedom, and elation.

Pause to notice the harmony of the four elements within you. Open your eyes, and conclude with the following prayer (*Nayaz*):

Beloved Lord, Almighty God!
Through the rays of the sun,
Through the waves of the air,
Through the All-pervading Life in space,
Purify and revivify me, and, I pray,
Heal my body, heart, and soul.
Amen.

PIR ZIA INAYAT-KHAN is the son and successor of Pir Vilayat Inayat-Khan, and the grandson of Hazrat Inayat Khan, the first Sufi master to bring Sufism into the West. In addition to the interfaith mystical training he has received from his father, Pir Zia has also studied Buddhism under the auspices of His Holiness, the Dalai Lama, and Sufism in the classical Indian tradition of the Chishtiyya Order. He holds a doctorate in Religion from Duke University, and is currently president of the Sufi Order International. Pir Zia is the author of *Saracen Chivalry: Counsels*

on *Valor, Generosity and the Mystical Quest,* and editor of *A Pearl in Wine: Essays in the Life, Music, and Sufism of Hazrat Inayat Khan,* as well as *Caravan of Souls: An Introduction to the Sufi Path of Hazrat Inayat Khan.* He lives with his wife and two children at The Abode of the Message in upstate New York and currently teaches Sufism around the world.

THE EXAMINATION OF CONSCIENCE

Sheikh Muhammad Jamal al-Jerrahi

O you who believe, be in awe of Allah and look well into yourselves to see what you have in stock for tomorrow.
  — *Qur'an 59:18*

Take account of your actions before Allah takes account of you, weigh yourself before you are weighed, and die before you die.
  — *Hadith, Al-menhajo'lqawwah*

MUHASABA IS A time-honored spiritual practice used to account for one's daily behavior and to scrutinize one's hidden motivations and tendencies as they manifest in everyday life. While the Arabic word, *muhasaba*, means to 'audit' or 'inspect' the balance of one's accounts, as a spiritual practice it refers to the examination of conscience, the weighing of one's deeds, and the accounting of the *nafs* (the ego, or limited self). *Muhasaba* is also a station on the mystic path in which the seeker may become established through persistence in the practice of self-examination.

The great Sufi mystic, Ibn al-Arabi informs us that in the early days of Islam, many of the pious would write down or memorize their thoughts, words, and deeds during the day in order to identify and repent of any sinful acts they may have committed. In this way, they endeavored to check their vanity and monitor any lapses into heedlessness. Such practices were also common among the Christian desert fathers and later the Kabbalists of Eastern Europe. One Hasidic *rebbe* (master) was known for writing down all his misdeeds during the day, then weeping until his tears of contrition fell and washed away the ink.

One of the most famous Islamic practitioners of this way of

self-accounting was Harith al-Muhasibi, an early Sufi master of Baghdad (781-857) who was a teacher of Pir Junayd al-Baghdadi, and who may be considered one of the first psychologists of Sufism. He encouraged reason over emotionalism, and eschewed all self-deception. He taught the "science of hearts," relying on the conscience in the depth of the heart *(sirr)* to correct the self-gratifying tendencies of the ego—the *nafs al-ammara* or 'commanding self'—through the practice of self-examination. By observing and correcting the often unconscious actions and motivations of the lower self, and the animal impulses arising from it, one begins to learn about one's own nature and gradually reign in and train the excesses of the *nafs,* so that its energies may be redirected toward divine service.

Through the benefits of *muhasaba*, one can progress beyond the unbridled self-indulgence of the *nafs al-ammara* to the next level of *al-nafs al-lawwama*, the 'self-blaming' or repentant self. At this stage, the spiritual aspirant, having become dissatisfied with the immature behavior of the lower self, repents and attempts to control its sensual appetites, self-indulgence and greed. Muhasibi taught that through diligent practice and divine grace, the baser qualities of the *nafs* may ultimately be transcended or transformed, so that the soul's innate wisdom can emerge, opening one to the pure station of the peaceful soul, *al-nafs al-mutma'inna*. At that stage, one is no longer ruled by the passions of the lower nature but is animated by the divine qualities and wisdom which shine forth with the purification of the heart and training of the *nafs*.

We should note that in Sufism, with its seven levels of the soul, the model is not to 'kill the ego,' but to train and transform the *nafs al-ammara*, so that it becomes no longer fixated simply on its own narcissistic gratifications, but learns to lend its energies in the service of the higher self and greater good. In this way, the realized soul gradually cultivates divine friendship, and the limited human will begins to merge with the divine will. When this unification dawns and the eye of the heart opens, one no longer sees others with the eyes of separation, but sees all creation as part of the One Reality and is caught up in the waves of divine love. Every being that comes before one is reverenced as the Beloved, and is understood mystically as an extension of oneself. Then, one is really able, as Christ said, to "love one's enemies, as (being) oneself." When we find ourselves grabbing for the largest slice, or cutting off someone in traffic, we understand that this ideal has not yet penetrated to the core of our being, and we may benefit from the practice of *muhasaba*.

In his 11ᵗʰ century spiritual classic, *The Alchemy of Happiness (Kimia-ye Sa'adat)*, Imam al-Ghazzali describes the practice of *muhasaba*, saying: "Just before going to sleep each night, the devotee should take account of what his *nafs* has done during the day . . . examining his motivation carefully." Like an accountant keeping a ledger, one is advised to divide one's behavior into three categories: meritorious deeds, neutral actions, and any negative actions which fall below the soul's ideal. In balancing the account, one aims to find enough positive deeds to outweigh the negative deeds. With each review one is discovering more about one's own nature, the negative as well as the positive qualities. One is reading the book of oneself, which is the most valuable book one can read.

The practice of *muhasaba* may also entail a period of reflection upon waking in the morning, accompanied by a resolve to refrain as much as possible from negative manifestations and to accentuate acts of generosity and goodness for the sake of *Allah*. A further extension of *muhasaba* is to strive to maintain a state of vigilance continually throughout the day, so that one's automatic behaviors and reactions become more conscious, and so that negative impulses may be observed and tempered as they arise, before they progress into the realm of destructive action. If one notices carefully, one may observe an impulse at the moment when it arises in heart. For instance, one might experience an impulse to retaliate for some offense, but also an impulse to let it pass and forgive, or to deflect the offense with humor. If one is awake and guarding one's behavior, the negative impulse, which is coming from the lower self, may be stopped at that point, as one needn't act on every impulse that arises. If it is not stopped there, then the impulse is quickly transmitted from the heart to the mind where thought brings judgment to bear on what action to take; then from thought, it moves through the body into the realm of action. One may then lash out, answer from the ego with a harsh word, or one may choose to check one's negativity with a sweet word or a noble silence. As the *Qur'an* (7:201) states in more religious language: "when a passing stroke from Satan troubles them, [they] immediately remember *Allah*, and lo! They are aware."

Sheikh Muzaffer al-Jerrahi explains: "The rule is, one is not responsible for the impulses which cross one's heart. Even if you were to intend to do something evil and then decided against it and refrained, instead of deserving punishment for it, you will be rewarded." This ties in with the divine principle of recompense as recorded in the *Qur'an* (6:160), which reveals that *Allah*, Most Merciful, only counts a mistake or evil deed once, but counts a good deed ten times, thus making it easier for us.

In respect to the accounting of the *nafs*, one may ask: by what standard does an individual judge between what is right and wrong? For the basics of moral and ethical guidance, we can consult the *Qur'an* or other revealed scriptures, as well as the *sunna* (tradition) of the Prophet and direct divine supplication. But for many of the more nuanced decisions in our daily lives we must look within and use the faculty of personal conscience. Hazrat Inayat Khan says:

> Conscience is a faculty of the heart as a whole, and the heart consists of reason, thought, memory, and the heart itself. The heart, in its depth, is linked to the divine Mind, so in the depth of the heart there is a greater justice than on the surface; and therefore there comes a kind of intuition, inspiration, knowledge, as the inner light falls upon our individual conception of things. Then both come together. In the conscience God Himself sits on the throne of justice.[44]

The principle of conscience and personal integrity is, as Shakespeare said in *Hamlet,* "To thine own self be true . . . and [then] thou canst not be false to any man;" or, as revealed by the Prophet Muhammad in a *hadith,* "He who knows himself knows his Lord." While each person's conscience and inner ideal may vary from culture to culture, shaped and influenced as it is by personal experience as well as genetic and societal influences, what is vital is to be in touch with one's own ideals, life-goals and deep principles and stay true to them as our sacred trust. Otherwise, if one betrays one's own conscience, the conscience itself will condemn one, filling the heart with self-reproach and eroding one's courage. The sincere lover of Truth sees every action as coming from the Ultimate Source and turns only to that Source for help, praying to be among those who flourish under the divine blessing, and to be protected from falling into errors which would

44 Inayat Khan, *Sufi Teachings,* 201.

initiate a chain of destructive consequences and close the heart to its own innate divine inspiration and radiance. This is the subtle meaning of *taqwa*, roughly translated as the fear of God or divine awe—that we would be continually sensitive in our life's decisions and actions, to signs indicating either divine permission and acceptance, or warnings that it is better for the soul to avoid certain thoughts and actions.

There are tendencies in our nature that are best handled by avoiding them or upgrading them through sublimation. There are other qualities such as compassion and joy, which we can nurture and spread, like watering a garden. By increasing awareness through *muhasaba*, we can guard against habitually watering the weeds of harmful or unworthy attitudes and actions, especially the tendency to despise or look down on others. The noble Prophet, peace and blessing be upon him, said to a follower named Anas: "Son, if you are able, keep your heart from morning till night and from night till morning, free from malice towards anyone." If we find that the grooves of the mind habitually run toward criticizing others (and by extension oneself), we can work to overwrite these grooves with new neural paths by emphasizing attitudes of generosity, gratefulness, forgiveness and acceptance, and consciously bring these into actuality through good deeds. Even a smile or an encouraging word to another counts. Then, when we review the activities of the day, we will begin to find the balance shifting toward more acts of beauty in our daily life. If at first, we seem to be more in touch with the personal surface emotions of the heart, with its unexamined likes, dislikes, resentments and past wounds, it only means that we have to dig deeper past the muddy ego-encapsulated regions until at last we reach the living spring of divine inspiration and love in the center of the heart, which is our connection with the divine heart.

Besides monitoring one's behavior, the practice of *muhasaba* can include self-questioning, with the aim of uncovering various unconscious motivations and conditioned attitudes. Such queries could function to open a revealing inner dialogue. For example: What expectations did I bring to the situation (and were they realistic)? Am I in touch with my life's purpose; and if so, is a given action in keeping with that purpose? If I am caught in some negative mode of thinking or acting, what is the true divine impulse that was originally intended but is not yet realized? The

Qur'an makes it clear that this life is a university for the education of souls, and that every day in which we do not learn or progress is a lost opportunity. Grappling seriously with such questions and monitoring our day-to-day experience can certainly accelerate our understanding of life and our place in it.

Ultimately, in self-examination, it is our conscience that acts as a barometer of our spirit; and the most basic litmus test of the rightness of an action is to consider whether the activity makes the heart feel positive or negative, uplifted or degraded, and whether it increases the soul's light or diminishes it. It is like a red light or green light in the center of the chest. If the conscience is ignored or overridden consistently, a rust forms on the heart that veils the inner light and distorts our understanding, isolating us further in the fiction of our separate ego identity. Fortunately, there are other practices in addition to *muhasaba*, which can help clear away the rust from the heart and bring us to union, such as *zikr*—divine remembrance—and *tafakkur*, mystic contemplation. Through all of these practices, the soul is given a key to find the hidden treasure, to awaken to the divine inheritance within oneself and in all the creation.

And We shall show them Our signs on the horizons and within themselves until it be manifested to them that it is the Truth.

> — *Qur'an* 59:18

Sheikh Muhammad Jamal Al-Jerrahi (Gregory Blann) has been an active student of Sufism and the world's religions for over three decades. He received a degree in music and art from Peabody College at Vanderbilt University in 1974. He was initiated by Pir Vilayat Khan in the Sufi Order International in 1980, serving as a representative in that order for a number of years. In 1990, he received initiation in the Halveti-Jerrahi Order from Sheikh Nur al-Jerrahi (Lex Hixon), and also began to study with Sefer Efendi in Istanbul, becoming a Jerrahi *sheikh* himself in 1994. He worked closely with Sheikh Nur for several years, translating the traditional mystic hymns of the Jerrahis from Turkish into English, to be sung by dervishes in the West. In recent years, Sheikh Muhammad Jamal has authored two books on Sufism: *The Garden of Mystic Love: Volume I: The Origin and Formation of the Great Sufi Orders*, and *Lifting the Boundaries: Muzaffer Efendi and the Transmission of Sufism to the West*. He has also been a frequent participant in ecumenical dialogues and panels, serving on the board of the Interfaith Alliance of Middle Tennessee. Sheikh Muhammad Jamal lives in Nashville, Tennessee and teaches Sufism locally and in various cities throughout the United States.

The Path of Radical Remembrance

Sheikh Kabir Helminski

For the Sufi, the remembrance of God always and everywhere is the aim of existence. But Who or What is God, and what is 'remembering'?

Is human language capable of expressing, or at least pointing toward, the reality of this word *God*? Some people—especially those who prefer a purely existential or scientific worldview—become disturbed when this word is used. Others become complacent and self-righteous. Perhaps it is better to be somewhat disturbed by the idea of God, especially if the disturbance causes us to crack the shell of our fixed concepts. Whatever God is, God is not one of our fixed concepts.

One cannot be a human being and not wonder about the real significance of being an individual, a person with self-awareness. Each us has a flame of consciousness at our core. What is the nature of this flame, and what kindled it within us? This consciousness is the most startling fact of our existence, and at the same time it is most often taken for granted.

It is said in our tradition: "You are God's secret. And God is your secret." To the gnostic, God is to be known through the flame of consciousness. To remember God is to be aware of that flame of consciousness. But we can only be aware of that flame *through* that flame. This is the paradox in which duality dissolves.

The flame of consciousness exists in us because consciousness permeates the universe. But the word *consciousness* implies something mental, abstract, almost impersonal. What if that flame is not only a flame of consciousness but also a flame of infinite qualities? What if fire not only contained heat and light, but love, creative power, and infinite intelligence?

What then if the human being could become aware of this inner flame as a spark of infinite creativity and love? What if the activation of our essential human qualities depended on our awareness of a spiritual connection to the Source of Life? This is the central premise of our work. Is this religion? Is this psychology? Is this art? Is this just common sense? Is it called becoming a complete human being? It doesn't matter.

> *Remember Allah, as He has guided you.*
> — *Surah al-Baqarah (2):198*

This deceptively simple statement enjoins us to remember and suggests that we have been "guided" to this remembrance by God. *Remembrance* is a translation of the Arabic word *zikr*, which has a number of meanings, including 'mentioning' and 'remembering.' *Remember* can be traced back to Middle English and Old French and comes from the Latin *rememorari*. To remember, however, is not simply the calling up of something from the past, but a calling to mind, a state of retaining something in one's awareness. We are reminded to remember by the One who instilled remembrance in us. This Qur'anic verse, this *ayat*, is a thin veil over the oneness of Being: our remembering is His remembering.

For the Sufi this remembrance has an essential nature beyond forms, which can be practiced anywhere and anytime.

> *And remembrance is the greatest.*

> *And God knows all that you do.*
> — *Surah al-'Ankabut (29):45*

REMEMBRANCE THROUGH THE NAMES OF GOD

Zikr has its specific forms, or exercises, which lead to experiences on levels within our own being. Al-Ghazzali, one of the greatest formulators and interpreters of Sufism, gave these instructions regarding the practice of remembrance:

> Let your heart be in such a state that the existence or non-existence of anything is the same—that is, let there be no dichotomy of positive and negative. Then sit alone in a quiet place, free of any task or preoccupation, be it the reciting of the Qur'an, thinking about its meaning, concern over the

dictates of religion, or what you have read in books—let nothing besides God enter the mind. Once you are seated in this manner, start to pronounce with your tongue, "Allah, Allah" keeping your thought on it.

Practice this continuously and without interruption; you will reach a point when the motion of the tongue will cease, and it will appear as if the word just flows from it spontaneously. You go on in this way until every trace of the tongue movement disappears while the heart registers the thought or the idea of the word.

As you continue with this invocation, there will come a time when the word will leave the heart completely. Only the palpable essence or reality of the name will remain, binding itself ineluctably to the heart.

Up to this point everything will have been dependent on your own conscious will; the divine bliss and enlightenment that may follow have nothing to do with your conscious will or choice. What you have done so far is to open the window, as it were. You have laid yourself exposed to what God may breathe upon you, as He has done upon his prophets and saints.

If you follow what is said above, you can be sure that the light of Truth will dawn upon your heart. At first intermittently, like flashes of lightning, it will come and go. Sometimes when it comes back it may stay longer than other times. Sometimes it may stay only briefly.

The method of attaining the "Truth" begins with this simple and beautiful practice of repeating "*Allah*," the essential name of God. Just by moving the tongue with a certain intention and presence of mind, we are taken into the reality of the Name until "only the palpable essence or reality of the name will remain, binding itself ineluctably to the heart." Through this simple process, the remembrance is transferred from the tongue to the mind, from the mind to the feelings and the deeper levels of the personality, until its reality is established in the core of the human being.

More and more, remembrance begins to fill one's life. Instead of the usual inner dialogues, commentaries, judgments, and opinions that make up the majority of people's inner life, we may begin to experiencethebreathandrhythmofremembrance.Thedivinenames are seen to be alive, animate, spiritually prolific—much more real than the repetitive scripts of our superficial personality.

This path requires no exceptional leap of faith, no abandonment of reason, no complex theology or intellectual attainment. The simple, mindful invocation of God's essential name will take us to the reality of what is being remembered.

REMEMBRANCE OF THE HEART

The remembrance that begins with the tongue can guide us to the remembrance of the heart. Perhaps it is evidence of the divine generosity that what begins with the simple repetition of a word could lead to the Secret of secrets, the innermost core of the heart. The repetition of the word *Allah* focuses our thought on God. The rhythm of remembrance inevitably affects brainwaves, and the superficial layers of the mind are calmed. In this transparent stillness of the superficial mind, a deeper level of mind becomes revealed. It is that deeper level of mind, called heart, which is capable of perceiving 'something' that is apparent neither to the intellect nor to the senses. It seems as if becoming aware of this 'something' has the effect of clarifying the mind, harmonizing the emotions, enhancing the senses, and bringing peace to the heart.

> *Truly, in the remembrance of God hearts find rest.*
> *— Surah al-Mu'minun (23):28*

> *And contain yourself patiently at the side of all who invoke their Sustainer, mornings and evenings, seeking His face, nor allow your eyes to go beyond them in search of the attractions of this world's life, and pay no attention to any whose heart We have made unaware of all remembrance of Us because he had always followed his own desires, abandoning all that is just and true.*
> *— Surah al-Kahf (18):28*

Westerners who are familiar with various spiritual paths may ask, "What is the difference between *zikr* and meditation?" If by meditation is meant that refined 'listening within,' the activation of a presence capable of witnessing inner and outer events without becoming absorbed in them, then there is much in common. We can, however, distinguish *zikr* from the more superficial techniques of concentration. Remembrance is more than an exercise performed for individual purposes such as attaining calmness, clarity, or relaxation. While *zikr* must include that state of concentration, it is more than that. Remembrance of God is establishing a relationship with infinite Being, which is both nearer to us than ourselves and, at the same time, greater than anything we can conceive. It is also experienced as loving and being loved by Love.

I once received a letter from a person who was in the midst of years of intensive practice within what he described as a "nontheistic tradition." During a three-year solitary retreat he began to practice a Sufi *zikr* using the name *Allah*. He described how in all his years of spiritual practice, and despite the many benefits of his practice, his heart had not found rest. "Perhaps there is something in approaching a God who can be named. My heart, for the first time, has found rest." Little did he know that he was quoting the *Qur'an* almost verbatim. Is his experience valid, or is it merely settling for some lesser satisfaction? Our understanding of remembrance is that the Divine has the qualities of indefinable transcendence, as the nontheistic approaches emphasize, and at the same time the Divine has a personal, intimate aspect, which is experienced as profound relationship.

While the invocation of the names or attributes of God is a primary practice, this remembrance can and should permeate the entire range of human capacities and activities. The *Qur'an* commends those who *remember God standing, sitting, and lying on their sides* (*Surah al-'Imran* 3:191), meaning under every possible circumstance. Every cell of the body longs to be in this state of remembrance. Sufism has many practices that allow remembrance to be incorporated at the bodily level: the standing, bowing, and prostration of the ritual prayer, *salah*; the whirling ceremony of the Mevlevi dervishes; the movements of the group zikrs of various Sufi orders.[45]

Sheikh Kabir Helminski began his study of Sufism with Sheikh Suleyman Loras of Konya and was officially recognized as a sheikh of the Mevlevi

[45] This article was excerpted with permission from Kabir Helminski's *The Knowing Heart: A Sufi Path of Transformation*, 96-101.

Order of Sufism in 1990, by the late Celalettin Celebi, head of the Mevlevi Order. From 1980 until 1999 he was the director of Threshold Books, one of the foremost publishers of Sufi literature. Between 1994 and 2000, he toured with the whirling dervishes of Turkey, bringing the spiritual culture of the Mevlevis to more than 100,000 people. For more than thirty years, Helminski's focus has been developing and sharing a contemporary approach to Islamic concepts and practice, practice, both within the Islamic community and outside of it. In 2001 he was the first Muslim to deliver the prestigious Harold M. Wit Lectures on Spirituality in Contemporary Life at Harvard Divinity School. Today, he is Co-Director of the Threshold Society and a core faculty member of the Spiritual Paths Institute. He is the author of two books on Sufism: *Living Presence* and *The Knowing Heart*.

THE PRAYER OF LIGHT

Sheikha Camille Adams Helminski

Upon awakening, the Prophet Muhammad would offer this prayer:

"We have awakened
and all of creation has awakened for God,
Sustainer of all the worlds.
God, I ask You for the best the day has to offer,
opening, support, light, blessings, guidance,
and I seek refuge in You from any harm in it
and any harm that might come after it."

He encouraged this opening to light also through a prayer he would recite after the morning *salat*. Following his example, Mevlana Jalaluddin Rumi also used to recite this same prayer each morning, and Mevlevi dervishes following their example have been reflecting on it daily for almost eight centuries now.

One might include this prayer in one's daily practice after some moments of prayer or silent meditation, awakening to the flowing of the breath. As one repeats the verses of the Prayer of Light, bring the attention to each area around and within the body as it is mentioned. With each breath, with intention wash the body with light even as one might with water. Bring awareness to the cleansing power of light, the healing power of light, the illuminative power of light, even deep within us.

Prayer of Light
1. O God! Grant me Light in my heart, Light in my grave,
2. Light in front of me, Light behind me,
Light to my right, Light to my left,

Light above me, Light below me,
3. Light in my ears, Light in my eyes,
Light on my skin, Light in my hair,
Light within my flesh, Light in my blood, Light in my bones.
4. O God! Increase my Light everywhere.
5. O God! Grant me Light in my heart,
Light on my tongue, Light in my eyes, Light in my ears,
Light to my right, Light to my left,
Light above me, Light below me,
Light in front of me, Light behind me,
and Light within my self; increase my Light.[46]

Duãunur

1. 'Allahummaj'al li nuran fi qalbi wa nuran fi qabri.
2. Wa nuran bayna yadayya wa nuram min khalfi
wa nuran 'an yamini wa nuran 'an shimali
wa nuram min fawqi wa nuram min tahti.
3. Wa nuran fi sam'i wa nuran fi basari
wa nuran fi sha'ri wa nuran fi bashari
wa nuran fi lahmi wa nuran fi dami wa nuran fi 'izami.
4. 'Allahumma'zim li nuran waj'alni nuraa.
5. 'Allahummaj'al fi qalbi nuran
wa fi lisani nuran wa fi basari nuran wa fi sam'i nuran
wa 'an yamini nuran wa 'an yasari nuran
wa min fawqi nuran wa min tahti nuran
wa min 'amami nuran wa min khalfi nuran
waj'al li fi nafsi nuran wa 'zim li nura.

---

46 Excerpted with permission from *The Mevlevi Wird,* translated by Camille Helminski with assistance from Cuneyt Eroglu, Mahmoud Mostafa, and Amer Latif, 67.

Learning this prayer by heart is a beautiful way to bring it close, and to be able to deeply refresh yourself each morning with the welcoming of Light. Within the Islamic tradition, there are Ninety-Nine Names of God that are commonly reflected upon, though it is understood that God is Infinite, Ultimately Un-nameable and beyond comparison with anything, that Source of Life is also intimately experienced, closer than our jugular vein. One of the traditional Ninety-Nine Names is 'The Light,' *An-Nur.* So in invoking Light *(Ya Nur,* 'O You who are Light') breath by breath, we are invoking the illuminative Presence of the Divine, opening to that Infinite Source of Being that gives us Life, that One Who enlightens our being and our Way, Light upon Light, *Nur ala nur.*

CAMILLE ADAMS HELMINSKI has been working within the Mevlevi tradition of Sufism for over thirty years. She is Co-Director of the Threshold Society, a organization dedicated to facilitating the direct personal experience of the Divine. With her book, *Women of Sufism,* she has helped increase awareness of the integral contribution of women to the spiritual path of Islam. She has co-translated a number of volumes of Sufi literature, including *Jewels of Remembrance* (excerpts of the *Mathnawi* of Jalaluddin Rumi), and is the first woman to translate a substantial portion of the Qur'an into English: *The Light of Dawn,* selections from the Qur'an for daily contemplation. She has authored two anthologies for the Book Foundation (www.thebook.org), *The Book of Character,* and *The Book of Nature, A Sourcebook of Spiritual Perspectives on Nature and the Environment.* Her most recent publication is *Rumi's Sun, The Teachings of Shams of Tabriz.*

Jewish Practices

BREATHING THE DIVINE NAME

Rabbi Jeff Roth

FOR THIS PRACTICE, we will make an explicit link to the most holy name for God in the Jewish tradition, *Yud Hay Vav Hay,* also called the *tetragrammaton.* These syllables are the names of the four Hebrew letters that comprise this most holy name, *Y-H-V-H.* The letter yud has the sound of the English letter *y.* The letter *hay* corresponds to the English *h.* The letter vav is like the letter *v* in English. The Jewish mystical tradition gives us a framework for understanding these four letters of God's name. Let's begin with the letter *hay,* or *h.* As you may have noticed, this letter appears twice in this name for God. If you intone the letter out loud, you will immediately recognize that it is the sound of breathing. Try this: breathe out loudly enough for an extended time so that you can hear the sound of the breath with your own ears. Now, if you do the same thing when inhaling, you'll hear that the in-breath also makes the same sound. The perspective that pronouncing the letter *hay* is the same sound as breathing makes an explicit link between the breath and God's name.

It may not come as a surprise that God's name is connected to the breath. Most religious traditions connect breath with life and with God. The English word *spirit* is related to the word *respiration.* In Hebrew, the words for 'soul' *(neshamah)* and 'breath' *(nesheemah)* have the same root. *Ruah* means 'spirit' in Hebrew, but it is also a word for the wind, or the movement of air, which is like the breath. In Genesis 2:7, when God wanted to make human beings, God breathed into the dust of the earth: "And *Y-H-V-H,* God, formed the human, of the dust from the soil, he blew into his nostrils the breath of life and the human became a living being." So when we pay attention to the breath, it is a way of paying attention to the divine animating life-force, which is inherent in each breath while we are still alive.

We have looked at two of the letters (the second and fourth) in the divine name, *hay* and *hay*. The other letters of the divine name provide different insights into the nature of God. The first letter is the *yud*. In Hebrew, this is the smallest letter of the alphabet and when written, its essence is the same as a single point. Since a point has no dimensions in time and space (its scientific definition), we need to draw something bigger than a point so that it can be seen. But Jewish mystics have always understood that the *yud* is connected to the concept of nothingness or emptiness. If we make a link to the breath, as we did for the letter *hay,* then we might consider that the *yud* in God's name corresponds to the state of emptiness that occurs before the in-breath begins. At that point, as the lungs have emptied of air, they contract, like a deflating balloon. While they do not disappear into nothingness, they do get to be their smallest size. Similarly, *yud* does not disappear, but is the smallest letter. If *yud* represents the empty place before the start of the in-breath, then the first *hay* in the divine name corresponds to the in-breath itself.

At the end of the in-breath, before the start of the out-breath, the lungs are now in their most expanded state. This can be called the full state. This full state can be linked to the Hebrew letter *vav*. *Vav* is the straightest letter in the Hebrew alphabet, written as simply a single straight line. To again use the image of a balloon, picture the long, skinny balloons used by people who make balloon animals. Before you start blowing it up, it hangs down, out of your mouth. As you blow it up, it straightens into a single straight line. In this way, vav can be thought of as fullness. Just as the lungs are full at the end of the in-breath.

We can now see that the whole cycle of breathing is coded within the divine name *Yud Hay Vav Hay,* as follows:

Yud—Empty
Hay—In
Vav—Full
Hay—Out

BREATHING AND THE DIVINE PRESENCE

To begin the practice of concentrating on your breath, sit comfortably in a quiet place where you won't be disturbed. Turn off the ringer of your phone. You might begin this and any formal practice session by making the following intention: the act I am about to perform, I do for the sake of waking up to the Divine Presence that pervades all life, in order that I might become an aide in helping all beings to awaken and live in peace and joy.

As you begin to sit quietly, start by noticing whatever thoughts or feelings are present in your mind before you pointedly direct your attention anywhere. After a few moments of this, begin to focus your attention on the arising and passing of each breath. Allow the breath to come and go at its own pace. Don't try to manipulate the breath in any way. See if you can make the primary object of focus the physical sensations that accompany the breath. At the same time, softly begin to connect in your mind the four parts of the breath to the four letters of God's name. When you feel the bodily sensations that are present after the emptying of air from your lungs, silently say to yourself, *"Yud."* As you notice the in-breath arising and the accompanying bodily sensations, say to yourself, *"Hay."* You might extend the inner noting of the word *hay* to cover the whole period of the in-breath. When the in-breath finishes, try to feel the sensations in your body that are present before the out-breath begins, and say to yourself, *"Vav."* As the out-breath begins, say to yourself, *"Hay,"* and extend that noting as long as the out-breath is occurring. Continue to feel the physical sensations in your body as you breathe out.

Repeat this pattern of connecting the letters of the divine name to the parts of your breath for ten minutes. While we begin with the intention to aim and sustain the attention on the object of focus, it is inevitable that your mind will wander. Try not to worry about it or judge yourself. Judging yourself discourages you from practicing because you feel "You're not good at it." It doesn't mean you are a bad meditator; it is just the nature of our minds to be distracted. When you find your attention wandering, simply bring your focus back to your breath and the connection to the divine name. This returning of the attention back to the object of focus is central to concentration practice.

You only need to cultivate the practice of noticing as soon as possible when your attention has wandered. And when you notice that, make a decision to return. This is a skill that can be developed over time. Eventually, you will notice that your ability to sustain your attention on the object of focus will grow. But don't expect your progress to be overly linear in development. Some days your ability to sustain your attention will be better than others. This may be true over periods of weeks or months as well, depending on many other factors that affect your life. For example, you might be less able to sustain your attention during times of life stress than in calm times.

You may find that you continue to judge yourself when your attention wanders. If so, you can work with this in your meditation. When you notice self-criticism, simply file this awareness away for future exploration. This is an example of concentration and awareness coming together. Negative self-judgment is one of the biggest impediments to waking up. For one thing, it makes us feel badly about ourselves, which is not very helpful when it comes to staying in the present moment. Ultimately, cultivating an attitude of self-acceptance is a crucial component of the growth that occurs as you see clearly the challenges you face in trying to be more awake in your life. Indeed, self-acceptance is a precursor to the deep happiness that is possible through this practice.

You might want to undertake this practice daily while working with this book, especially, if you just beginning to explore meditation. But it may be that using the names of the Hebrew letters *yud, hay, vav,* and *hay* is too abstract for you. In that case, consider using the words *empty, in, full,* and *out* instead. English words may resonate for some people more than the Hebrew letters. You might try the practice each way and see which words better help you sustain your attention to the breath.[47]

RABBI JEFF ROTH is one of the primary teachers of The Awakened Heart Project for Contemplative Judaism, promoting the use of Jewish contemplative techniques that foster the development of a heart of wisdom and compassion. He was also the co-founder of Elat Chayyim Jewish Renewal Retreat Center, which he served as Executive Director and Spiritual Director for 13 years. He is an experienced meditation

---

47 Excerpted with permission from Rabbi Jeff Roth, *Jewish Meditation Practices for Everyday Life: Awakening Your Heart, Connecting with God,* Jewish Lights, 2009: 26-27, 29-30.

teacher, a facilitator of Jewish meditation retreats, and the author of *Jewish Meditation Practices for Everyday Life: Awakening Your Heart, Connecting with God.* For more information on the Awakened Heart Project, see www.awakenedheartproject.org.

The Practice of Self-Understanding

Rabbi Zalman Schachter-Shalomi

I WANT TO INTRODUCE YOU to a subtle and powerful meditation technique from the Habad Hasidic tradition, called *hitbonenut* (self-understanding). This technique is sometimes done in the course of one's daily prayers, or separated from them as an independent practice. It is a special technique of discursive meditation or contemplation, during which one thoroughly explores a spiritual concept, filling one's consciousness with it and thus brings about change in one's life.

At first, we think about the idea or concept in an objective way, attempting to understand it intellectually, down to its very last detail. But when we have finished filling-out the concept and have mastered the thought-sequence in all its rich detail, we should then move into the dimension of situational-thinking. That is to say, we must re-invest the conceptual material with a real-life-context.

This situational mode of thought is called *ada'ata d'nafshei* in the Jewish tradition, and fills us with an immediate emotional awareness, and even provokes us to action. For example, we might fully understand what it means for someone to inherit a large sum of money, considering the situation and all its various ramifications, such as the personal, social, and societal effects of a sudden acquisition of capital. Now, imagine *you* are the *actual* beneficiary, right now, in this moment, *ada'ata d'nafshei*, finding yourself filled with emotion that begets a corresponding response in behavior. From this, you can immediately see just how vital *ada'ata d'nafshei* thinking can be to your meditation.

God Fills All Worlds: A Meditational Dry Run

Now let's begin our practice with a traditional meditation on the

Divine Indwelling in Creation. This idea is spoken of as *M'malleh Kol Almin*, God's 'Filling all Worlds' with Light and Life.

Most people generally have a notion of there being a God 'out there,' 'somewhere' in the universe. And it is possible to construct a conceptual framework within which one might think about God in this way. But, as the *Tikkunei Zohar* says, "There is no thought that can take hold of You." Thus, in time, we find ourselves at a loss, trying to think about God, and yet knowing the futility of such an approach. Nevertheless, the *Tikkunei Zohar* continues, "but the Infinite God is taken hold of by the longing of the heart."[48] The longing of the heart is something that is not reaching toward an *idea*, but toward a *Presence* and a *Being*.

You see, when the "longing of the heart" takes over, we are no longer dealing with the God-*idea* in the third person; we are dealing with the second-person *Presence* of the Living God. Here, I find myself alive in the Divine *milieu*. I am not talking *about* God, I am speaking to . . . *You, O Life, O God, O Knower, O Beloved. I know that I am shaped and created by Your Love, and the very words that are rising in my mouth, and the feelings rising in my heart, are not my creation, but are made, focused, fielded, and made possible by You!*

So we meditate on God 'filling our universe' with life, and we do this *ada'ata d'nafshei*. We are now, here, filled with Life, with God. We wonder at our own being, at our own body; this amazing biological factory, converting oxygen and food into consciousness and life. Our pulse is beating and our vitality fills us with curiosity. You see, reveling in this field that is not held together by our volition but by the grace of God holding us in life, is a way of getting to know God as immanent in Creation.

But we, in our little selves, are only tiny parts of this great universe, *v'olamot ain mispar*, "the Worlds without number." There are Worlds that are so short-lived, like muons and pions, fractions, millionths of a second, and Worlds that are so vast that our galaxy itself pales beside them. Thus, we can begin to see the vastnesses of these vibrations in which a whole life can happen in a millionth of a second, or so slowly that one circuit of the Sun takes 226 million years! Each of these is 'filled' by God. So, when I speak of God, and think only of the vast and expansive God, I sometimes fail to recognize God in the infinitesimal life of a muon. We must

---

48 *Leit mahshava tefisa bah klal . . . aval nitfas ihu be-reuta de-liba.*

remember that *Divinity fills all Creation, great and small!*

When we face this tremendous fact, we feel something in our hearts; but that feeling is not as important as *Whom* we feel. When we reach this point in our meditation, we must hold on to it. In this, we face and behold God. As the emotion subsides, the subtlety of the meditation deepens, and form gives way to formlessness. It is at this stage that we allow the Divine in without reserve, and allow its power to re-orient our souls.

Now, relax and continue in the flow this meditation for a moment, as I do a little of it with you:

All is filled with life. Wherever we turn, life abounds. The All vibrates in Song. Every individual cell is filled with life, as is every atom. All of life proceeds from a Source. "For with You is the source of Life, in Your Light do we see Light." Life makes things live.

The Life is hidden in the things It invigorates. It cannot show Itself to them, lest they cease functioning as living beings. To faint is to be overwhelmed by one's life. If one's life leaves, one cannot live. Thus Life must hide Itself in the very thing it gives life to.

All of life is in continuous motion, moving to and fro, vibrating in harmony. Life is the effulgence of the Infinite. Like sunlight proceeding from the Sun, without effort on the part of the Sun, so does the Light of the Infinite proceed to reflect God. Everything alive basks in God's Radiance.

You are now being filled like a pitcher plunged in the sea, filled with water on the inside and surrounded by oceans of water without. In all your functions, picture them in detail, going through these functions in your mind, picturing yourself being filled with Life. As you realize that even in times of life-denial you are still filled with this Life, you come to feel remorse. But you shouldn't turn fully in this direction at this moment. Rather, visualize yourself being filled by God and all the Worlds (from the highest to this, the lowest) being filled by God. You are also to visualize God in your work and recognize that God fills your day, the vehicle you drive, the room you are in, in the very place you are standing or sitting.

All this Life that surrounds you, challenges you to fulfill its wish to be reflected back to God. The very sidewalk says to you: "Cleave to God, to God's Torah and Mitzvot, or else with what right do you step on me?!" The food you eat, (so full of life) also wishes to be reflected back to God. It, and every desirable and enjoyable thing, says to you: "Reflect me back to God! Do not see in me only an end, but rather as a means to express God as God fills me and surrounds me."

Now say to yourself, "God is always near me, nearer than the feeling I now feel." This beholding of Life filling the All bestows great joy. There is no despair, no loneliness, for God is always in us and in all things.

This is a very important concept in Habad Hasidism, and one worth exploring, but you should feel free to branch-out, exploring other spiritual ideas in the same way, *ada'ata d'nafshei*, experiencing them personally and allowing them to transform you from the inside out.

Moreover, this practice takes deepening and repeating, over and over again. When I was a young man in the *yeshivah* (seminary), my *mashpiyya* (mentor) would insist, "Repeat, repeat, repeat." The Hasidic master, Reb Pinhas of Koretz put it this way: "The soul is an indifferent teacher . . . It doesn't repeat anything twice." Therefore, we have to help the soul by ruminating on the experience, repeating the sequence over and over again. Remember, soul-craft calls for diligent, careful and caring work in the garden of mind.

RABBI ZALMAN SCHACHTER-SHALOMI (d. 2014), better known as Reb Zalman, was born in Zholkiew, Poland, in 1924. His family fled the Nazi oppression in 1938 and finally landed in New York City in 1941. Descended from a distinguished family of Belzer Hasidim, he became a Habad Hasid as a teenager while still living in Antwerp, Belgium. He was later ordained by Habad-Lubavitch in 1947 and became one of the Lubavitcher Rebbe's first eneration of outreach workers. He later earned his M.A. in psychology from Boston University in 1956, and a D.H.L. from Hebrew Union College in 1968. He was professor emeritus of Psychology of Religion and Jewish Mysticism at Temple University and World Wisdom Chair holder emeritus at Naropa University. The rebbe and father of the neo-Hasidic Jewish Renewal movement, he was generally considered one of the world's foremost authorities on Hasidism and Kabbalah. Schachter-Shalomi was the author of *Spiritual Intimacy: A Study of Counseling in Hasidism, Jewish with Feeling: Guide to a Meaningful Jewish Practice*, and co-author of *A Heart Afire: Stories and Teachings of the Early Hasidic Masters*.

Pouring Your Heart Out to God

Ozer Bergman

Then the Rebbe put his arm around my shoulder and said, "And also, it's very good to pour out your heart to God as you would to a true, good friend."

— Rabbi Noson of Nemirov

WITH THESE WORDS, the great Hasidic master, Rebbe Nachman of Breslov introduced to his major disciple, Reb Noson, the practice that is the backbone of Breslov Hasidism—*hitbodedut*. The literal meaning of *hitbodedut* is 'self-seclusion.' The externals of *hitbodedut* are easy to describe. You choose a time which is convenient for you to devote to talking to God. You decide how much time you want to spend talking to God. You find a place where you will be undisturbed for the desired period. When the appointed hour comes, you show up and talk to God in your own words, in your native tongue, about whatever you want. Ideally you will continue every day—day in and day out—for the rest of your life.

Starting and maintaining a daily practice of *hitbodedut,* like starting and maintaining any endeavor, requires a number of internal externals: determination, courage, youthfulness, perseverance, audacity, joy, optimism, trust, patience, and enthusiasm. Moving further inside, we note that *hitbodedut*, like many spiritual practices, requires faith—in one's teacher, in one's self, and in the practice. At its core, *hitbodedut,* like all religious devotions, requires faith in, and a nearly unquenchable desire for God.

"Why should I talk to God? And what would I say?" The answer to the first question is what the holy Zohar posits as the *raison d'etre* of Creation: to know God. The more you talk to God about your fears, frustration, pain, pleasures, hopes, aspirations, and concerns; the more you discuss your theological difficulties, your appreciation for things great and small, and your love for God, the more you know God. And the more the world exists on account of you.

What will you say to God? Rebbe Nachman offers two suggestions. The first is to attach yourself to what touches your heart *now*, today. This is an aspect of self-review, looking honestly and objectively at your behavior towards others, towards yourself and towards God. No one is perfect. Something in our life is certainly broken, and many times we are the one who broke it. So this aspect of *hitbodedut* calls for self-reproof, for the sake of self-correction. The point of the self-correction is to stay centered and on course, so that you don't stray from the goal of knowing God. Sometimes an aspect of your temperament may be disconnecting you from your focus. For example, you might talk about your bad temper:

God! My fuse is way too short. Almost every little thing sets me off and ruins my equilibrium. What's worse though, is my reaction! Words that shouldn't be said, tantrums that shouldn't be had, throwing stuff! I break things and ruin my relationships with people—some of whom I actually like!

Please help me. Remind me that You are in charge of the world—not me. Remind me that You've got a plan, and that You're in the details; that it's okay, or even better than okay, if things don't go my way. I'm not a baby anymore. Help me to be mature and to behave more maturely.

You are a microcosm of Creation. By fixing what's broken in you, you fix everything. Nevertheless, the results of *hitbodedut* are not always immediate. In some areas of life, it may take years to make serious progress. But never give up!

When you choose this method of getting in touch with your heart, probing its sensitivity today, you generally end up with a session of *hitbodedut* that flows wherever your courage lets it. However, the other method Rebbe Nachman recommends results in a much more structured, perhaps even detailed, *hitbodedut*. Rebbe Nachman calls this "turning Torah into prayer."

This is exactly what it sounds like: as you learn a piece of Torah—Written or Oral, revealed or esoteric—in addition to the information you absorb, you also keep track of your current level of faith, as well as the ethical and practical lessons that the text is providing you. Compare your current spiritual status with that towards which the text beckons you. Some works need a fair amount of decoding in order to figure out the destination and how to get there. Others, such as Rebbe Nachman's *Likutey Moharan*, provide a basic road map outlining an order of steps you might take to reach higher levels of spiritual integration. For example, in Lesson 23 of *Likutey Moharan*, Rebbe Nachman teaches us that various aspects of the commandment to affix a *mezuzah* (parchment scroll inscribed with selected verse from Deuteronomy) on your doorpost allude to sexual morality, the desire for money, contentment, honest business practices, as well as travel. From that you might come up with the following in your *hitbodedut*:

God, thank You for helping me to honor this commandment, for making it so easy. I hang it up once, and I'm keeping it 24 hours a day, 7 days a week! Let me be cheered by the sight of it, knowing that You've helped me accept Your invitation to be part of my home.

I've heard that our Sages teach, and Rebbe Nachman re-emphasizes, that the commandment of affixing a mezuzah can also help me overcome my acquisitive desire, and not be jealous of others. Help me to remember that, so I can own my possessions, instead of the other way around. Help me to undo my thoughts of jealousy and the things I did wrong as a result. May such thoughts never again hold sway over me.

Please protect my body, soul, money, and possessions from all harm and damage, from theft, robbery and loss.

May the holiness of the commandment of affixing a mezuzah become part of me as I come and go. May its merit protect me wherever I travel, so that I leave home and return home in peace and safety.

May I be inspired by the commandment of affixing a mezuzah to holiness and generosity, and may that holiness and generosity bring a long, joy-filled life in their wake. May they also save me from disagreements, both spiritual and material, and from enemies, and may there be peace in the world.

In yet another teaching, Lesson 7 of *Likutey Moharan*, Rebbe

Nachman relates the commandment of wearing *tzitzit* (ritual fringes which remind us of the commandments) to faith, sexual morality, and taking advice. From this, you might pray something along these lines:

Dear God—

May the corners which hold my tzitzit become wings, shielding me from temptation—in particular, the mirage of sexual desire—allowing me to become holier.

May the corners which hold my tzitzit become wings, carrying me closer to You. May my new found holiness help me recognize and refuse bad advice, advice that is ultimately harmful and destructive. Help me and protect me from smooth-talkers and good-lookers, even if their intentions are innocent.

Let my mind be clear and unencumbered by the transient things of life so I can understand correctly the advice of the righteous, so that the choices I make will be true and intelligent.

At many points on your journey these methods will synchronize. You will then begin to realize that *your life is Torah* and the *Torah is your life*. Everything in the Torah is meant to shine God's light on everything you experience, and your every experience is meant to shine your Godly light on the Torah. *Amen.*

OZER BERGMAN was born in Brooklyn, New York, and earned his B.A. from Johns Hopkins University and rabbinic ordination from the Bostoner Kollel in Jerusalem. In addition to writing and translating for the Breslov Research Institute, he is one of the editors responsible for making Rebbe Nachman of Breslov's multi-volume work, *Likutey Moharan* available in English. He is also the author of *Where Earth and Heaven Kiss: A Guide to Rebbe Nachman's Path of Meditation.*

Taoist Practices

THE BREATH OF TAO

Kenneth Cohen

OF THE THREE GREAT teachings (*san jiao*) of ancient China—Confucianism, Buddhism, and Taoism—only Taoism may be called an indigenous Chinese religion. Confucianism is a philosophy that emphasizes ethics and social harmony. Buddhism searches for the cause of suffering through meditation and introspection. It is an import from India and had to adapt to pre-existing Taoist philosophy and monastic customs. But Taoism is essentially Chinese, a combination of even earlier shamanism, called *wu jiao* in Chinese, and spiritual practices established by mountain hermits. These hermits were drawn to the beauty, power, and peace of nature. Some were former government employees who escaped from the chaos, intrigue, and aggression common during the early centuries B.C.E.. If they were successful in their quest for a deeper truth, they merged with the spirit of nature, achieved health and longevity, and became the realized sages that in Taoism are known as 'Immortals' (*Xian*).

Why is this tradition called Taoism? It is based on the Tao, literally a 'road' or 'trail.' The Tao is the path of nature and naturalness. The goal of Taoism is summarized in the opening line of the *Tao Te Ching* (Classic of the Tao and Its Virtue), written by the philosopher Lao Tzu in the fourth century B.C., "The Tao that can be spoken of is not the Tao." Why can't you speak about the Tao, the Way of Nature? Because you are it! There is no outside perspective. Humans may think and act as though they are separate from nature, and thus have the right to manipulate it without consequence, but is this really true? Are we supernatural or even unnatural? I don't think so. You can no more talk objectively about the Tao than you can use a sword to cut itself or lift yourself up by your own bootstraps. The Tao is where words begin: subject undivided from object. What is that which produces thoughts, what is that state of silent being from which words arise?

To answer this question is a logical impossibility.

Additionally, because life, the Tao, is always changing, how can words, which require fixed definitions, ever represent it? If you can capture the wind or flowing water in a bucket, then you can describe the Tao! The Tao that can be described is not the Tao, because the mystery of nature must be experienced. It flows and changes from moment to moment.

Thus, observation and meditation are central to understanding Taoism. Taoist monasteries are *guan,* "observatories," places to observe nature and one's inner nature. To observe accurately requires freeing the mind of preconceptions, prejudices, and cultural filters. A Taoist must cease being a Taoist; he or she must *un-know.* "The scholar seeks to gain day by day, "writes Lao Tzu, "the Taoist seeks to lose day by day. Losing and losing until reaching the effortless state where nothing happens *(wu wei)!"* The mind returns to its roots. Lao Tzu continues, "Use the outer light to return to insight." Complexity returns to simplicity. Existence itself merges with the great emptiness where no division exists. This is not the emptiness of nihilism, as though the world loses its meaning. Just the contrary—emptiness is the freedom of space, where there are no ruts to follow and all possibilities exist. It is a kind of mental suppleness.

We find a beautiful summary of these ideas and of the essence of Taoist meditation in chapter 40 of the *Tao Te Ching:*

> *Reversal is the movement of the Tao;*
> *Suppleness is the function of the Tao.*
> *Under heaven, all things are born of being;*
> *And being is born of Emptiness.*[88]

There are many forms of Taoist meditation, including visualizations to realize the unity of microcosm and macrocosm; *qigong* (life-energy) meditations to clear the acupuncture meridians of obstructions; methods of absorbing life-force from the sun, moon, and stars; and internal alchemy to combine the interior subtle energies and create the "golden elixir" of health and wisdom. In this chapter, I will teach you two of the most classic and revered Taoist meditations, called "embryonic respiration" and "whole body breathing." The goal is learn to breathe innocently and deeply like a newborn baby. Breath is a reminder that life is not a possession. We allow nature as air into the body; we let it go. Breathing teaches us to surrender to the wisdom of the Tao as manifest in our body's natural rhythms. In chapter 10 of the *Tao Te Ching,* Lao Tzu says:

> *Controlling the yang and yin, embracing the One.*
> *Can you not allow separation?*
> *Concentrating the qi, attaining suppleness,*
> *Can you become like a child?*

EMBRYONIC RESPIRATION

Find a time in the morning or evening when you will not be disturbed. Sit on a cushion on the floor or on a chair. Wear comfortable clothes. Loosen your belt if you need to. The back is straight but not stiff. Your lower body feels rooted into the ground, and your head is lifted slightly towards the sky. You are relaxed, using minimal effort to maintain an elegant posture. To encourage healthy breathing, it is especially important to release the chest and the abdomen. Neither lift nor depress the breastbone. The lower abdomen, between the navel and pubic bone, is free of tension and fully capable of moving as you breathe. This may take patience and practice, as many people unconsciously hold the belly in or try to make it appear flat. This interferes with breathing and makes one energy-starved. Once you have learned these various techniques and no longer need to follow the instructions, try the meditations with the eyes lightly closed. Lower the eyelids as though gently lowering a curtain.

Stage 1: Deep Breathing: Shen Hu Xi

Breathe slowly, silently, and naturally. When you inhale through the nose, the belly gently expands. When you exhale through the mouth, it releases, effortlessly. With each inhalation imagine that you are drawing-in the pure energy of the universe. It spreads through your entire body, refreshing and renewing you. With each exhalation, you release the old, unneeded energy. Do this for ten breaths, silently counting your exhalations.

Stage 2: Gathering Life-Force: Cai Qi Fa

From this stage onwards, all of your breathing, inhalation and exhalation, is through the nose (unless you have a nasal or sinus obstruction, in which case adjust as needed). Continue with abdominal breathing, inhaling the belly expands; exhaling it lets go. Remember, don't exert force, trust nature to move your breath without your help!

As you inhale, imagine breath energy goes to the center of the chest near the breastbone, as though you have a small energy reservoir there. As you exhale, imagine the breath drops down from the chest to the lower abdomen, to a reservoir about 1.5 inches below the navel and about three inches inwards (in the direction of the lower back). This lower reservoir is called the *dan tian,* 'the elixir field.' Practice ten repetitions. Every inhalation brings *qi* to the chest; every exhalation drops the *qi* into its storage tank, the abdominal *dan tian.*

Stage 3: Internal Breathing: Nei Hu Xi

Continuing with silent abdominal respiration, in and out through the nose, as you inhale imagine that the breath is an internal current of *qi* (life-force) that rises from the *dan tian* to the chest. As you exhale, the breath drops from the chest back down to the *dan tian.* Thus, although you are, of course, continuing to breathe naturally, in your mind the breath is entirely an internal current of energy. Inhaling, breath rises from abdomen to chest. Exhaling, breath descends from chest to abdomen. Up and down, up and down, ten repetitions. This method is sometimes called "the mixing of fire (heart) and water (kidneys)."

Stage 4: Effortless Breathing: Wu Wei Hu Xi

Continuing, now keep your mind on the gentle opening and closing of the abdomen as you inhale and exhale. When you inhale, don't suck the breath in. When you exhale, don't push the breath out. Discover the natural pace of your breath. Get out of the way and don't interfere. Can you be aware of the four stages of breathing: 1. the way breath comes in; 2. the turning of the breath between inhale and exhale; 3. the exhalation; and 4. the natural pause that occurs at the end of the exhale before breath comes back in?

Pay attention to these stages for a few minutes. The points of the turning of the breath between inhale and exhale and again between exhale and inhale are between *yin* and *yang*. They are gateways to stillness. If you allow all four stages, never deliberately sucking, pushing, or holding the breath, your breathing rate will slow down. Practice for about five to ten minutes. This stage flows naturally into the next.

Stage 5: *Embryonic Respiration:* Tai Xi

Now the breath seems to neither rise nor fall, neither open nor close. It is so ultra-slow and soft that if a down feather were held in front of the nostrils, it wouldn't move. Your mind merges with the breath, as though the breath is your entire world. The belly is pleasantly warm. You are like a mother nurturing her womb with caring, compassionate awareness. You are breathing like a baby in the womb of creation. Enjoy as long as you wish (or if you must look at a clock, I suggest twenty to thirty minutes).

Whole Body Breathing: Zheng Ti Hu Xi

Follow the same 'Basics' described at the beginning of Embryonic Respiration. Now imagine that the body is so open, so light, so receptive, that every cell is breathing (which, scientifically speaking, is true). With each gentle inhalation, your whole body is refreshed. Fresh *qi* goes to the skin, the muscles and tendons, the nerves, the internal organs, the joints, the bones. There is no place that can resist the breath. And with every effortless exhalation, every tissue and cell lets go of what it no longer needs. The breath is a gentle breeze, and every part of your body is a sail that can respond to it. Taoists say that a sage can breathe with the feet. Can you breathe with your feet, with your ears, your fingers, the crown of your head? What do you need to adjust so that your whole body is breathing? Practice for ten to fifteen minutes or for whatever period feels comfortable.

Closing & Opening Words

Breath is life. Breath is Tao. We can survive for a long time without food or water; but deprived of the invisible air, we count our lives in minutes. No wonder all of the world's religions acknowledge its importance. It is *qi* in Taoism, *prana* in Hinduism, *ruah* and *ruh* to Jews and Muslims, *pneuma* to the Christians, and acknowledged with a myriad of other names by the indigenous peoples of Africa, Australia, and the Americas. If only the world's religious leaders would remember that we all breathe the same air, the pathway to peace would be obvious.

KENNETH COHEN (GAO HAN) is a well-known Qigong Master and Taoist scholar/initiate. He was a student and friend of Alan Watts and former apprentice to Taoist Abbott Huang Gengshi. Cohen is the author of *The Way of Qigong: The Art and Science of Chinese Energy Healing* (Ballantine Books), *Taoism: Essential Teachings of the Way and Its Power* (Sounds True audio), and more than 200 articles on spirituality and health. He is the founder and director of the Qigong Research and Practice Center (www.qigonghealing.com).

PART II
SELECTED READINGS FROM THE
WORLD'S SPIRITUAL TRADITIONS

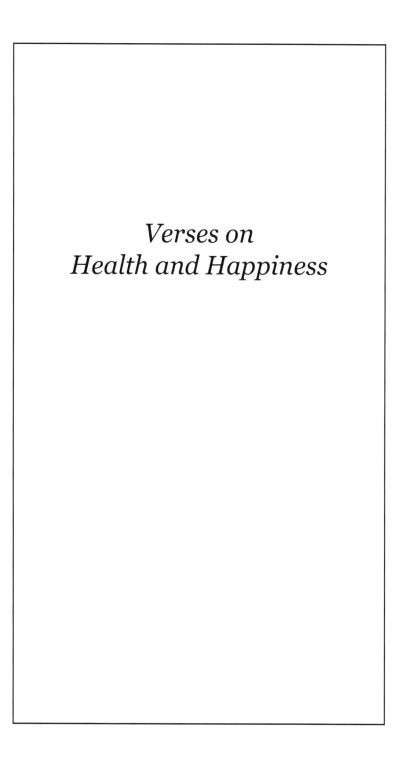

*Verses on
Health and Happiness*

BUDDHISM

May all beings everywhere,
Plagued by sufferings of body and mind,
Obtain an ocean of happiness and joy
By virtue of my merits.

May no living creature suffer,
Commit evil or ever fall ill.

May no one be afraid or belittled,
With a mind weighed down by depression.

May the blind see forms
And the deaf hear sounds.

May those whose bodies are worn with toil
Be restored on finding repose.

May the naked find clothing,
The hungry find food.

May the thirsty find water
And delicious drinks.

May the poor find wealth,
Those weak with sorrow find joy.

May the forlorn find hope,
Constant happiness and prosperity.

May there be timely rains
And bountiful harvests.

May all medicines be effective
And wholesome prayers bear fruit.

May all who are sick and ill
Quickly be freed from their ailments.

Whatever diseases there are in the world,
May they never occur again.

May the frightened cease to be afraid
And those bound be freed.

May the powerless find power
And may people think of benefiting each other.
— Bodhicharyavatara[1]

CHRISTIANITY

The prayer offered in faith
Will make the sick person well;
The Lord will raise them up.

If you have sinned, you will be forgiven.

Therefore, confess your sins to each other
And pray for each other
So that you may be healed.
— James 5:15-16

May the God of hope
Fill you with all joy and peace
As you give your trust
So that you may overflow with hope
By the power of the Holy Spirit.
— Romans 15:13

HINDUISM

For a hundred autumns may we see,
For a hundred autumns may we live,
For a hundred autumns may we know,
For a hundred autumns may we rise,
For a hundred autumns may we flourish,
For a hundred autumns may we be,
For a hundred autumns may we become,
— and even more than a hundred autumns!
— Atharva Veda XIX, 67

Instill in us a wholesome, happy mind
With goodwill and understanding.

Then shall we ever delight in your friendship
Like cows who gladly rejoice in meadows green.

This is my joyful message.
— Rig Veda X, 25:1[2]

INDIGENOUS SPIRITUALITY

When you have that chanupa [pipe],
You have to be humble and sincere.

You ask for health *and* help.

These are the two key words
That the chanupa *carries.*
— Wallace Black Elk, Lakota Shaman

Tunkashila [God], *from these powers*
I have to speak from my heart.

Come pity us and have mercy upon us.

You know we are a pitiful people.

Give us health *and* help
Because we don't know anything.

We made some mistakes,
So please forgive us.

Let us do something good
To replace the mistakes we made.
— Wallace Black Elk, Lakota Shaman[3]

Islam

In Surat al-Fatihah
There is a balm for all ailments.
— Muhammad, *Rasul Allah*[4]

Surely, the friends of Allah
Will have nothing to fear,
Nor will they need to be sorrowful.

Those who believe and lead a righteous life,
For them there is happiness,
Here, and in the Hereafter.

Such is the inviolable law of Allah;
This is the mighty triumph!
— Qur'an 10 (Surat al-Yunus):62-64

Judaism

Bless the Lord, O my soul,
All my being, bless the holy Name.

Bless the Lord, O my soul,
And do not forget the many bounties
Of the One who forgives all your sins,
And who heals all your diseases,
Who redeems your life from the Pit,

Who surrounds you with steadfast love and mercy,
Who satisfies your years with good things,
So that your youth is renewed like the eagle.
— Psalms 103:1-5

Happy is the one who finds wisdom
And gains understanding.
— Proverbs 3:13

TAOISM

Health is the greatest possession.

Contentment is the greatest treasure.

Confidence is the greatest friend.

Non-being is the greatest joy.
— Unknown[5]

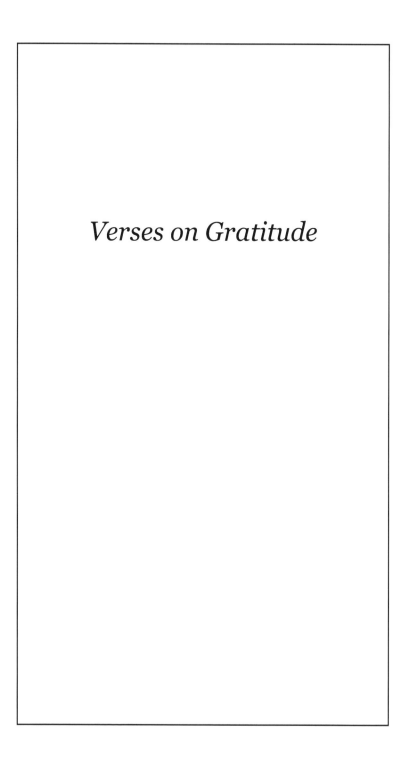

Verses on Gratitude

Buddhism

The unworthy person
Is ungrateful and forgetful.

This ingratitude, this forgetfulness
Is congenial to the unworthy.

But the worthy person is grateful
And mindful of all help.

This gratitude, this mindfulness,
Is congenial to the worthy person.
— Anguttara Nikaya I: 61

You, Universally Honored,
Are a great benefactor.

By doing this rare thing,
You have taught and benefited us
Out of your compassion toward us.

I will never be able to repay your favors,
Even if I try for millions of kalpas.

I will never be able to repay your favors,
Even if I bow respectfully to you,
Offering my hands or feet and everything else.

I will never be able to repay your favors,
Even if I carry you on my head or shoulders

And respect you from the bottom of my heart
For as many kalpas as there is sand in the River Ganges.
— The Lotus Sutra 4

CHRISTIANITY

Rejoice always;
Pray without ceasing;
In everything give thanks;
For this is God's will for you
In Christ Jesus.
—1 Thessalonians 5: 16-18

HINDUISM

When a person is born, whoever they may be,
There is born simultaneously a debt
To the gods, to the sages, to the ancestors,
And to other human beings.

When one performs sacrifice,
It is the debt to the gods that is concerned.

It is on their behalf, therefore, that one
Makes a sacrifice or an oblation.

And when one recites the Vedas,
It is the debt to the sages that is concerned.

It is on their behalf, therefore, that one recites,
For it is said that they are the guardians
Of the treasure store of the sages.

And when one desires offspring,
It is the debt to the ancestors that is concerned.

It is on their behalf, therefore, that acts,
So that their offspring may continue.

And when one entertains guests,
It is the debt to human beings that is concerned.

It is on their behalf that one entertains,
Providing food and drink.

The person who does all these things
Has performed a true work;
They have obtained all, conquered all.
— Satapatha Brahmana I, 7.2: 1-5[6]

INDIGENOUS SPIRITUALITY

To the Great Spirit's day;
To the center of that day
I will go and make an offering.

This I burn as an offering; behold it!
A sacred praise I will make. (twice)
The nation, may you behold it.

The path of the night-moon will be my robe.
The day-sun promised me a robe.
— Standing Bear, Lakota Elder[7]

Before Grandfather Sun comes up,
I arise to offer sacred smoke
And prayers to the Maker and Shaper.

I send my prayers on the wind, to the four directions.

I ask Creator to take pity on humanity
For we are seeking our correct path.

I enter the Silence.

I listen to the great guardians,
Trees, without whose breath we cannot live.

I offer prayers of gratitude to the plants and nature,
For it is through nature that we are guided to the Infinite.

Nature is the good spirit that guides us
And shows us how to live in harmony and balance.
— Tezkalci Matorral Cachora, Yoeme/Lacandon Maya[8]

ISLAM

Be grateful to Allah:
Whoever is grateful,
Profits in their own soul.

But if any is ungrateful,
Allah is still free from want
And worthy of praise.
— Qur'an 31 (Surat al-Luqman):12

JUDAISM

It is good to give thanks unto the Lord,
To sing praises unto Your Name, Most High,
To proclaim Your loving-kindness in the morning,
And Your faithfulness every night.
— Psalms 92: 1-2

TAOISM

*Mysterious ancestor of Heaven and Earth,
Original root of the ten thousand breaths.*

Cultivating the Tao *through countless ages,
Bear witness to my spiritual enlightenment.*

*Within and without the three realms of being
Only the* Tao *is revered.*

Golden light is shining down on me.

*Looking, it cannot be seen;
Listening, it cannot be heard.*

Embracing all of Heaven and Earth,
It nourishes all sentient beings.

Chanting sacred texts a myriad times,
The body develops a clear brilliance.

The three realms of being guard me;
The five lords of the elements welcome me.

I bow prayerfully to all sacred beings
And command the thunder spirits.

Ghosts and demons lose courage;
Sprites and goblins disappear.

Inside there is a crash of thunder;
Yet the thunder gods conceal their presence.

Cavernous wisdom, penetrating intelligence!

The five qi *are mounting on high!*

May the golden light quickly manifest
And protect the True Sage!

The Ruler of the Heavens commands
The golden light to descend! So be it!
— Golden Light Invocation[9]

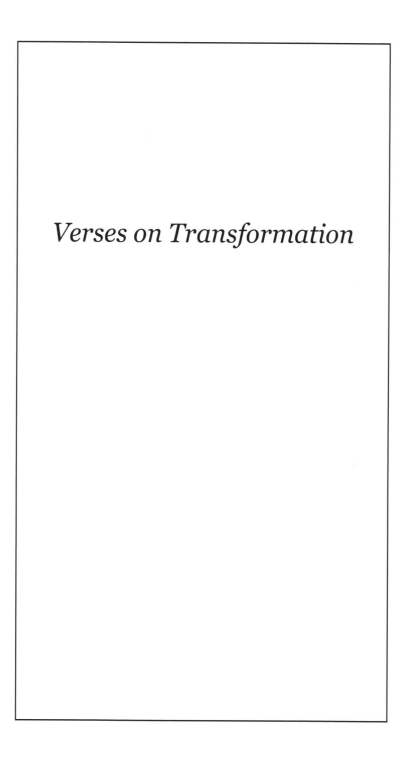

Verses on Transformation

BUDDHISM

All beings, without number, I vow to liberate;
Endless blind passions, I vow to uproot;
Dharma *gates beyond measure, I vow to penetrate;*
The way of the Buddha, I vow to attain.
— The Bodhisattva Vow

I hold all before my mind,
And to the mighty Sage, the greatest of our kind,
And to his heir, I make a perfect offering,
Sublime recipients, compassionate lords,
O think of me with love; accept these gifts of mine!

Deceived and overpowered by my ignorance,
I have taken pleasure in wrong doings,
And seeing now the faults in these,
O great protectors, I confess it earnestly.

Until the essence of enlightenment is reached,
I go for refuge to the Buddhas.

Also, I take refuge in the Dharma
And in all the host of Bodhisattvas.
— Bodhicharyavatara 2:6, 29, 26

CHRISTIANITY

There was once a man who had two sons.

The younger one said to his father,
"Father, give me my share of the estate."
So he divided his property between the two.

Not long after that, the younger son
Set off for a distant country with his wealth
And squandered all of it in wild living.

After he had spent everything,
There was a severe famine in that land,
And he began to be in need.

So he went and hired himself out
To a citizen of that country,
Who sent him to his fields to feed pigs.

He longed to fill his stomach
With the pods that the pigs were eating,
But no one gave him anything.

When he came to his senses, he said,
"How many of my father's workers have food to spare,
And here I am starving to death!

I will set out and go back to my father and say to him:
'Father, I have sinned against heaven and against you.

I am no longer worthy to be called your son;
Make me like one of your hired men.' "

So he got up and went to his father.

But while he was still a long way off,
His father saw him and was filled
With a mighty compassion for him.

He ran to his son,
Threw his arms around him
And kissed him in joy.

The son said to him, "Father,
I have sinned against heaven and against you.

I am no longer worthy to be called your son."

But the father said to his servants,
"Quick! Bring the best robe and put it on him.

Put a ring on his finger and sandals on his feet.
Bring the fattened calf and kill it.

Let's have a feast and celebrate.

For this son of mine was dead and is alive again;
He was lost and is found!"
— Luke 15:11-24

Ask and you will be given;
Seek and you will find;
Knock and the door will be opened;
For everyone who asks, receives;
Anyone who seeks, finds;
If only you will knock,
The door will be open.
— Matthew 7:7-8

HINDUISM

Just as a caterpillar,
Having reached the end of a blade of grass
And approaching another one, collects itself
[For making the transition],
Even so this atman, *having discarded*
The body and overcome ignorance,
Approaching another one
Collects itself [for making the transition].

Just as a goldsmith,
Taking an object of gold,
Fashions it afresh into another
New and more beautiful form,
So the atman, *discarding this body*
And dispersing its ignorance,
Makes for itself another
New and more beautiful form:
That of the Fathers, the spirits, the Gods,
Prajapati, Brahman, *or of other beings.*

This atman *is in truth* Brahman,
Consisting of consciousness,
Desire and desirelessness,
Righteousness and unrighteousness.

According to one's deeds,
According to one's behavior,
So one becomes.

The one who does good becomes good,
The one who does evil becomes evil.

One becomes virtuous by virtuous action
And evil by evil action.

But others say that
The human being consists of desire;
As is the desire, so is the intention,
And as is the intention, so is the action.

And whatever the action, that is what is obtained.
— Brhadaranyaka Upanishad, IV[10]

INDIGENOUS SPIRITUALITY

May you behold this —
I have asked to be made over;
May you behold this —
I have asked to be made over.

A good nation I have asked to be made over.

May you behold this —
I have asked to be made over;
May you behold this —
I have asked to be made over.

A sacred nation I have asked to be made over.

May you behold this —
I have asked to be made over;
May you behold this —
I have asked to be made over.
— Nicholas Black Elk, Lakota Shaman[11]

ISLAM

O you who believe!
Turn to Allah *with sincere repentance,*
Hoping that your Lord will
Remove from you your ills,
And admit you into Gardens
Under which rivers flow.

That Day Allah *will not disgrace the Prophet*
And those who believe with him.

Their Light will run forward before them
And with their right hands they will say:
"Our Lord! Keep perfect our Light for us
And grant us forgiveness;
For You are Able to do all things."
— Qur'an 66 (Surat al-Tahrim):8

JUDAISM

Nathan the Prophet
Had just been to scold David
Because he had come in to Bat Sheba,
And David cried out:

Please be gracious to me God,
Be kind to me.

With Your great compassion
Erase my guilt.

I know I was an offender,
My sin stares me in the face.

I failed You alone,
What You consider evil—
I have done.

I admit that You are right
Your judgment is just.

(Don't judge me harshly)
In the heat of passion
My mother conceived me.

Was I not fashioned in lust?

In my kidneys I feel Your scrutiny
You inform me in hidden thoughts —
Please scour me with hyssop
And I will come clean,
Scrub me to be as white as snow.

Let me hear joy and glee again
So the bones in me
That still hurt from Your rebuke
Will be able to delight again.

Turn Your face from my sins
Do wipe out all my wrong doings.

God! Create in me a clean heart
Renew in me a sensitive spirit.

Don't push me away from You,
Don't deprive me of Your Holy Spirit.

Let me regain the joy I felt
When You helped me
Support me in an attitude of generosity.

Let me teach the rebellious
What Your way is about;
Those who failed at virtue
I will bring back to You.

My caring God
Save me from bloodguilt;
Master! Give me back
My power to speak to You.

My very tongue is eager
To sing of Your fairness.

Then Your praise
Will flow from my mouth with ease.

If You really wanted sacrifices
I gladly would bring them;
But it is not a burnt offering
That You want from me.

Instead You favor
My humbled spirit, God,
My heart broken regret
You will not despise.

As for Zion; pour out Your good will
Raise up Jerusalem's buildings.

In that setting we will offer oblations
Of all kinds that You desire.

Then even cattle will be raised
To be Your altar.
— Psalm 51[12]

Taoism

1. Practice inaction and effortless flow (wu wei)
2. Be supple and soft;
3. Guard the feminine, and don't be first;

4. Be nameless;
5. Practice purity and tranquility;
6. Engage in only good and skillful behavior;
7. Practice desirelessness;
8. Be contented;
9. Yield and withdraw.
— Taoist Precepts[13]

*Verses on
Love and Compassion*

BUDDHISM

May I be a guard for those who are protectorless,
A guide for those who journey on the road.

For those who wish to cross the water,
May I be a boat, a raft, a bridge.

May I be an isle for those who yearn for land,
A lamp for those who long for light;
For all who need a resting place, a bed;
For those who need a servant, may I be their slave.

May I be the wishing jewel, the vase of wealth,
A word of power and the supreme healing,
May I be the tree of miracles,
For every being the abundant cow.

Thus, for everything that lives,
As far as are the limits of the sky,
May I be constantly their source of livelihood
Until they pass beyond all sorrow.
— Bodhicharyavatara 3:18-20, 22

CHRISTIANITY

Dear friends,
Let us love one another,
For love comes from God.

Everyone who loves has been
Born of God and knows God.

Whoever does not love
Does not know God,
Because God is love.

Dear friends, since God so loved us,
We also ought to love one another.

No one has ever seen God;
But if we love one another,
God lives in us and God's love
Is made complete in us.

We love because
God first loved us.

If anyone says, "I love God,"
Yet hates their brother,
They are liars.

We are given this command:
Whoever loves God must also love their brother.
— 1 John 4: 7-8, 11-12, 19-20, 21

HINDUISM

Love is the firstborn,
Loftier than the Gods;
You, O Love, are the eldest of all,
Altogether mighty.

To you we pay homage!

Greater than the breadth
Of Earth and Heaven
Or of Waters and Fire,
You, O Love, are the eldest of all,
Altogether mighty.

To you we pay homage!

Greater than the quarters and directions,
The expanses and vistas of the sky,
You, O Love, are the eldest of all,
Altogether mighty.

To you we pay homage!

Greater than all things moving and inert,
Than the Ocean, O Passion,
You, O Love, are the eldest of all,
Altogether mighty.

To you we pay homage!

Beyond the reach of Wind or Fire,
The Sun or the Moon,
You, O Love, are the eldest of all,
Altogether mighty.

To you we pay homage!

In many a form of goodness, O Love,
You show your face.

Grant that these forms may penetrate
Within our hearts.

Send elsewhere all malice!
— Atharva Veda IX: 2:19-21, 23-25[14]

INDIGENOUS SPIRITUALITY

Grandfather, the Great Spirit,
Behold me on earth.

It is said that you lived first.
You are older than all
The prayers that are sent to you.

All things on earth,
The four-leggeds, the wings of the air,
Belong to you.

It is said that you
Have made all things.

I will send up a voice in behalf
Of everything that you have made;
The Indians, you have made
Their ways to live;
They are in despair right now.
Therefore I will send a voice to you,
Great Spirit, my grandfather . . .

All the universe,
The stars and the heavens and the earth
And the four quarters you have set;
Day in and day out
All the winds of the air live
And the morning star
And all beings that
Walk the earth.

Thus I send a voice
In behalf of my people
And also my relatives-like
The four-leggeds
And the wings of the air,
Of the four quarters
And the powers you have set.
— Nicholas Black Elk, Lakota Shaman[15]

ISLAM

*My love belongs to those
Who love each other in Me,
Who experience intimacy in Me,
Who shower each other
With goodness for My Sake;
And who visit each other
Joyfully for My Sake.*
— Mishkat al-Anwar, Hadith 88[16]

JUDAISM

*Who is a God like You —
Forgiving transgression
And pardoning wrongs,
Not remaining wrathful
Against the remnant of Your people,
For You desire loving-kindness!*

*You take us back in love,
Covering up our transgressions in compassion,
Hurling our sins into the depths of the ocean.*

*You keep faith with Jacob and loyalty to Abraham
As You vowed to our forebears long ago.*
— Micah 7:18-20

Taoism

The Tao *arises from the study of the heart;*
Incense transmits the heart's wishes.

Incense burns in the jade stove;
The heart appears before the Great Lord.

The true spirits look down;
The Immortals cast their regal gaze.

Now the disciple's message
Has truly penetrated the Nine Heavens!
　　　— Offering Incense Chant[17]

*Verses on
Breathing and Mindfulness*

BUDDHISM

A bhikkhu *having gone to the forest,*
To the foot of a tree, or a solitary place,
Sits down cross-legged, the body erect,
And directs the mind to the object of mindfulness;
Then, with mindfulness, breathes in and breathes out:
Inhaling a long breath — "I inhale a long breath,"
Exhaling a long breath — "I exhale a long breath,"
Inhaling a short breath — "I inhale a short breath,"
Exhaling a short breath — "I exhale a short breath";
"Aware of this whole body of breath, I breathe in,"
"Aware of this whole body of breath, I breathe out,"
"Calming the process of breathing, I breathe in,"
"Calming the process of breathing, I breathe out,"
Thus does the bhikkhu *train awareness.*
— Mahasatipatanasutta

CHRISTIANITY

Truly, truly, I say unto you,
Except a person be born
Of water and of the spirit-breath,
They cannot enter into the kingdom of God.
— John 3:5

If you want to pray,
Enter your inner room,
Close the door,
And pray to your Father in secret,
And your Father who sees in secret
Will reward you.
— Matthew 6:6[18]

HINDUISM

Praise to the Breath of Life!
Who rules this world,
Who is the master of all things,
On which all things are based.

Praise to your uproar, Breath of Life!
Praise to your thundering!
Praise to your lightning!
Praise for your rain, Breath of Life!

When the Breath of Life with thunder
Roars over the plants,
Then the flowers, pregnant with pollen,
Do burst forth in abundance!

When the Breath of Life, in due season,
Roars over the plants,
All things on earth rejoice!

When the Breath of Life rains life
Across the breadth of the earth,
The cattle exult, saying, "We shall have plenty!"

The plants speak with the Breath,
Drenched in its moisture, "Our life is prolonged,
For you have made us all fragrant!"

Praise to your coming and your going, Breath,
Praise to your rising and your settling, Breath!

Praise to you, Breath of Life,
For both breathing in and out!
For turning to this side and to that,
Praise to all of you, everywhere!

Breath of Life, grant your blessed form
To us that we may live!
Give us your healing power!

The Breath of Life cares for all beings
Like a parent their child;
Master of all life, breathing or not.

We breathe in, we breathe out,
Even within the womb.
Quickened and enlivened by you,
And you bring us to birth!

Breath of Life, please do not forsake me.

You are, indeed, everything that I am.

As the embryo of all potential,
I bind myself to you that I may live!
— Atharva Veda XI, 4:1-10, 14, 26[19]

INDIGENOUS SPIRITUALITY

Behold me,
The four quarters of the earth,
Relative-like I am.

Give me the power to see
And the strength to walk
The soft earth, relative-like I have been.

Give me the eyes of power
And the strength of knowledge
So I may be like unto you.

With your strength
I may face the winds.

In facing the winds,
May you behold me.

May I have the power of the winds.
— Standing Bear, Lakota Elder[20]

ISLAM

Behold, the Lord said to the angels:
I shall now create the human being,
Out of potter's clay, shaped and formed
To receive the breath of my Spirit . . .
— Qur'an 15 (Surat al-Hijr): 28-29

JUDAISM

The heavens are shaped by Yah's Word,
Yah's breath gives life to all its being.
— Psalms 33:6

The Sovereign Lord says to these bones:
I will make breath enter you,
And you will come to life.
— Ezekiel 37:5

TAOISM

Empty yourself of everything.
Let the mind become still.

The ten thousand things rise and fall
While the Self watches their return.

They grow and flourish
And then return to the source.

Returning to the source is stillness,
Which is the way of nature.
— Lao Tzu, *Tao Te Ching,* 16[21]

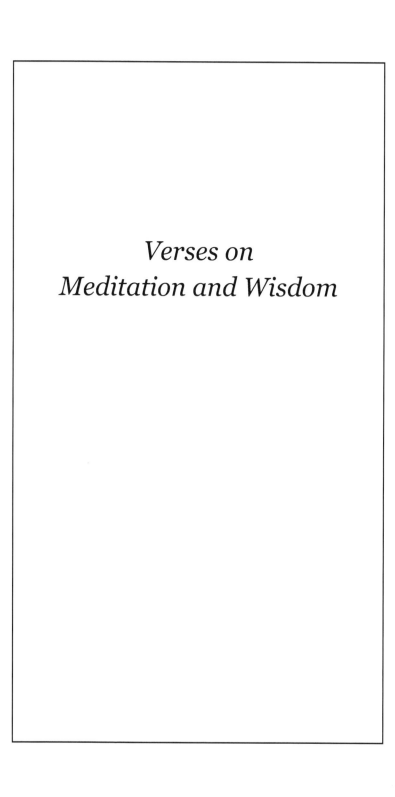

*Verses on
Meditation and Wisdom*

BUDDHISM

Just as a bird with undeveloped
Wings cannot fly in the sky,
Those without the power of higher perception
Cannot work for the good of living beings.

The merit gained in a single day
By one who possess higher perception
Cannot be gained even in a hundred lifetimes
By one without such higher perception.

Those who want swiftly to complete
The collections for full enlightenment
Will accomplish higher perception
Through effort, not through laziness.

Without the attainment of calm abiding,
Higher perception will not occur.
Therefore make a repeated effort
To accomplish calm abiding.

When the practitioner has gained calm abiding,
Higher perception will also be gained,
But without practice of the perfection of wisdom,
The obstructions will not come to an end.
— Atisha

CHRISTIANITY

*Ever since I first heard of
Your strong faith in Jesus, our lord,
And your love for God's people everywhere,
I have not stopped thanking God for you.
I pray for you constantly, asking God,
The glorious Father of our Lord Jesus Christ,
To give you spiritual wisdom and insight
So that you might grow in your knowledge of God.*

*I pray that your hearts will be flooded with light
So that you can understand
The confident hope he has given you,
His rich and glorious inheritance.
I also pray that you will understand
The incredible greatness of God's
Power for us who believe.
This is the same mighty power
That raised Christ from the dead
And seated him in the place of honor
At God's right hand in the heavens,
Far above any ruler or authority
Or power or leader or anything else,
Not only in this world
But also in the World-to-Come.*
— Ephesians 1:15-21

HINDUISM

"Instruct me, Sir."
Thus Narada approached Sanatkumara. [. . .]

"Contemplation, verily, is greater than thought.
For the earth, as it were, contemplates;
The atmosphere, as it were, contemplates;
Heaven, as it were, contemplates;
Water, as it were, contemplates;
The mountains, as it were, contemplate;
Gods and human beings, as it were, contemplate.

Therefore the one who attains greatness has,
So to say, a share in contemplation.

Small-minded people are
Quarrelsome, wicked, and slanderous,
Whereas the excellent have, so to say,
A share in contemplation.

Meditate on contemplation.

"One who meditates
On contemplation as Brahman,
Their freedom will extend to
The limits of the realm of contemplation,
One who meditates on contemplation as Brahman."

"But, sir, is there anything greater than contemplation?"

"Yes, there is something greater than contemplation."

"Then please, sir, tell me about it!"

"Wisdom, verily, is greater than contemplation.
For by wisdom one knows heaven and earth,
Air and atmosphere, water and fire,
Gods, human beings, and animals, grass and trees,
Right and wrong, true and false, pleasant and unpleasant,
Food and drink, this world and the other . . .

All these are known by wisdom.
Meditate on wisdom.

"One who meditates on wisdom as Brahman,
Attains the worlds of wisdom and of knowledge.

Their freedom will extend to the limits of the realm of wisdom,
One who meditates on wisdom as Brahman."
— Chandogya Upanishad VII, 6:1-7:2[22]

INDIGENOUS SPIRITUALITY

He he he hey (four times)
Grandfather, the Great Spirit,
You have been always,
And before you no one has been.

There is no other one
To pray to but you.

You, yourself, everything that you see,
Everything has been made by you.

The star nations all over the universe
You have finished.

The four quarters of the earth
You have finished.

The day, and in that day
Everything you have made.

On earth, everything
You have done.

Grandfather, Great Spirit,
Lean close to the earth
So you may hear the voice I send.

A nation we shall make;
Without difficulties we shall make it.

Toward where the sun
Goes down, behold me.

The Thunder-beings, behold me.
Where the Giant lives
There is power with the buffalo,
So I hear, behold me.

To where the sun shines continually
With the elks, behold me.

To where you always face,
A man with power, behold me.

To the depths of the heavens,
An eagle with power, behold me.

To mother earth, it is said
You are the only mother
That has shown mercy
To your children.
— Standing Bear, Lakota Elder[23]

ISLAM

There are those who remember God
Standing and sitting and reclining,
And who reflect upon the creation
Of heaven and earth.
— Qur'an 3 (Surat al-Imran):191

JUDAISM

I am continually with You,
You have grasped my right hand.

With Your counsel You guide me,
After glory You take me.

Who have I in heaven?

With You I have no desire on earth.

My flesh and heart fade away,
While God becomes the rock of my heart,
My portion forever. . . .

For me, closeness to God is good,
I have placed my essence in God my Lord,
To express all Your transcendence.
— Psalms 73:23-28[24]

Know that wisdom is sweet to your soul;
If you find it, there is hope
And it will not be cut off.
— Proverbs 24:14

TAOISM

Taos can be spoken about,
But not the Immortal Tao;
Names may be called,
But not Tao's name.

Not naming is the womb of heaven and earth.

Naming is the mother of all things.

Therefore ever without desire,
Contemplate the beginnings.

Ever with desire, see only the outcome.

These two are a merging,
But in issuing forth differ in name.

Merging—call it darkness and mystery.

Mystery beyond mystery,
The gateway to all wonder.
— Tao Te Ching 1[25]

Verses on Dedication

BUDDHISM

And now as long as space endures,
As long as there are beings to be found,
May I continue likewise to remain
To drive away the sorrows of the world.
— Bodhicharyavatara 10:55[26]

CHRISTIANITY

Lord, make me an instrument of Your peace;
Where there is hatred, let me sow love;
Where there is injury, pardon;
Where there is doubt, faith;
Where there is despair, hope;
Where there is darkness, light;
And where there is sadness, joy.

O Holy Master,
Grant that I may not so much seek
To be consoled, as to console;
To be understood, as to understand;
To be loved, as to love;
For it is in giving that we receive,
It is in pardoning that we are pardoned,
And it is in dying that we are born
To Eternal Life — Amen.
— Attributed to Francis of Assisi

HINDUISM

Be gracious, O Lord, to our approach,
Kindly as a friend, a father, or a mother.

Grant us Your treasure, liberal Lord,
Rich as You are when brightly enkindled.
With Your shining arms and flickering shapes
Convey it to the home of Your blessed singer.
— Rig Veda III, 18[27]

INDIGENOUS SPIRITUALITY

We have come on a good road
Of loving one another
And sticking by one another.

At this time we will disperse,
So keep the good work
And love one another.

That is the road that we came from,
The road of life,
Nothing but good,
And have strong will power
To do all this.

And all this, it will be so.
— Slow Buffalo, Lakota Chief[28]

In this world,
We walk along steep places.

If you move here and there,
How will you avoid falling?

Avoid extremes,
Keep to the middle way,
For only in the center
Lies the right social function,
The honorable condition.
— The Book of the Ancient Words[29]

ISLAM

My Mercy and Love are upon you, O Adam!

Go now to the gatherings where the angels are seated
And greet them with the words,
Salaam alaykum, *peace be upon you.*

The angels responded to Adam,
And may the Peace and Mercy of Allah
Also be upon you.
— Mishkat al-Anwar, Hadith 24[30]

All people belong to Allah's *family,*
And Allah *favors best those who are*
Useful to Allah's *family.*
— Muhammad, *Rasul Allah*[31]

JUDAISM

The Lord bless you and keep you;
The Lord deal kindly and graciously with you;
The Lord bestow favor on you and give you peace.
— Numbers 6:24-26

TAOISM

Don't exalt "superior" men
And the people will not contend.

Don't value goods hard to obtain
And the people won't turn into robbers.

Don't display the desirable
And the people won't be unsettled.

Therefore the sage governs
By emptying the mind
And filling the belly,
Weakening ambition,
And strengthening the bones.

Keep the people free from knowledge and desire,
And the wise guys will not dare to act.
Do without doing
Then all will be in order.
— Tao Te Ching 3[32]

INTERSPIRITUAL
DEDICATION

I. MAY WE BE HAPPY AND HEALTHY

In all the world
I cannot find
The source of peace
Outside my mind.

Neither play, nor drink,
Nor sex, nor food,
Can cause a constant
Blissful mood.

The things I see,
Touch, smell, taste, hear,
Cause both joy and pain,
Hope and fear.

Meditation relieves
my mind of stress,
Leading me to health
And happiness.

II. MAY WE BE GRATEFUL FOR LIFE'S MANY GIFTS

To all my teachers,
I beseech,
Please stay near
and help me teach.

You wisdom helped me
To find my way,
For constant blessings
I will always pray.

To the natural world
That sustains my living
I honor her
For always giving.

Life's bliss and pain
both provide
fertile fields
For wisdom's growth.

III. May We be Transformed into Our Highest Ideal

This ignorance does
A prison make,
Only true wisdom
Helps me escape.

My many faults
I now confess,
And clear them all
Through forgiveness.

Freedom lies
Inside, not out,
Of this pure truth
I have no doubt.

I know that
Real happiness
Must arise from my
Own consciousness.

Within my being's
Sacred design,
Resides the heart
Of the divine.

IV. MY WE BE LOVING AND COMPASSIONATE

For those who
Live in misery
I engage in
active empathy.

To help all creatures
To be free,
I place their joy
In front of me.

With love's
Compassionate intent,
I strive for pure
Enlightenment.

The only true
Pain prevention
Is my
Compassionate intention.

V. MAY WE BE MINDFUL THROUGH BREATHING

Mindfully my
Breathing starts,
My consciousness
Goes to my heart.

Within the silence
Of my breath,
There is no birth,
There is no death.

When thoughts
disturb the stillness,
I return
To emptiness.

And then I rest
With tranquil mind
In unity
With the divine.

VI. MAY WE BECOME WISE THROUGH MEDITATION

I rest into
A sacred presence
Joined as one
Eternal essence.

The silent wisdom
Keeps me seeing
The loving nature
Of my being.

Sacred light pervades
Me through and through,
And bliss descends
Like mountain dew.

Radiating out,
I now impart
Rainbows of healing
From my heart.

VII. MAY WE SERVE ALL BEINGS

I send love to friends
And foes who fight
To oppressors and
Oppressed alike.

I see the people
In my life
And vow to help
Overcome their strife.

I vow to sustain
This peace of mind,
To all I meet
I will be kind.

Liberation for all
Is my dedication;
May you be blessed
By this meditation.[33]

Notes on the Verses

1. A popular translation from the *Bodhicharyavatra* attributed to His Holiness, Tenzin Gyatso, the 14th Dalai Lama.

2. Reformatted adaptation from Raimundo Panikkar, ed. and trans., *The Vedic Experience – Mantramanjari: An Anthology of the Vedas for Modern Man and Contemporary Celebration,* 303, 302.

3. Reformatted adaptation from Wallace Black Elk and William S. Lyon, *Black Elk: The Sacred Ways of a Lakota,* 54, 118-19. There is a parallel reference to 54 on 102. The *chanupa* is the Lakota for the sacred pipe; it is the carrier of one's prayers. *Tunkashila* [toon-kash'-la] is the Lakota for the Grandfather aspect of the Creator.

4. Reformatted adaptation from Moinuddin Chishti, *The Book of Sufi Healing,* 159.

5. This saying is attributed to Lao Tzu, though this attribution is doubted by our contributor, Kenneth Cohen.

6. Reformatted, gender inclusive adaptation from Panikkar, *The Vedic Experience,* 393.

7. Reformatted adaptation from Raymond J. DeMallie, ed., *The Sixth Grandfather: Black Elk's Teachings Given to John G. Neihardt,* 287.

8. Original translation © 2010 by Grace Alvarez Sesma, used with permission.

9. Original translation © 2010 by Kenneth S. Cohen, used with permission.

10. Reformatted, gender inclusive adaptation from Panikkar, *The Vedic Experience,* 759.

11. Reformatted adaptation from DeMallie, *The Sixth Grandfather,* 126.

12. Original translation © 2010 Zalman M. Schachter-Shalomi, used with permission. The rest of the Jewish verses were adapted by the editor.

13. Original translation from the Lao Jun Jing Lu, *Precepts of Lord Lao Tzu* © 2010 by Kenneth S. Cohen, used with permission.
14. Reformatted adaptation from Panikkar, *The Vedic Experience*, 243-44.
15. Reformatted adaptation from DeMallie, *The Sixth Grandfather*, 294-95.
16. Reformatted adaptation from Muhyiddin ibn al-'Arabi, ed. and trans. Lex Hixon/Nur al-Jerrahi and Fariha Fatima al-Jerrahi, *101 Diamonds from the Oral Tradition of the Glorious Messenger Muhammad*, 141.
17. Original translation © 2010 by Kenneth S. Cohen, used with permission.
18. Thomas Keating, *Manifesting God*, 9-10. The rest of the Christian verses were adapted by the editor.
19. Reformatted adaptation from Panikkar, *The Vedic Experience*, 206-08.
20. Reformatted adaptation from DeMallie, *The Sixth Grandfather*, 286.
21. Reformatted adaptation from Lao Tsu, trans. Gia-Fu Feng, *Tao Te Ching*, 18. Only the first half of number 16 is given here.
22. Reformatted adaptation from Panikkar, *The Vedic Experience*, 676, 679.
23. Reformatted adaptation from DeMallie, *The Sixth Grandfather*, 286.
24. Reformatted adaptation from Aryeh Kaplan, *Meditation and the Bible*, 7.
25. Original translation © 2010 by Kenneth S. Cohen, used with permission.
26. Shantideva, trans. Padmakara Translation Group, *The Way of the Bodhisattva*, 169.
27. Reformatted adaptation from Panikkar, *The Vedic Experience*, 840-41.
28. Reformatted adaptation from DeMallie, *The Sixth Grandfather*, 312-13.
29. Original translation from *Libro de las Antiguas Palabras, Huehuetlahtolli* © 2010 by Grace Alvarez Sesma, used with permission. The Spanish is: *En este mundo caminamos por lugares escarpados. Si te mueves para acá o para allá, ¿cómo evitarás caer? Evita los extremos, mantente en el medio, pues*

sólo en el medio existe la función social, la condición honorable.

30. Reformatted adaptation from Ibn al-'Arabi, *101 Diamonds*, 65.

31. Reformatted adaptation from Javad Nurbakhsh, ed. and trans., *Traditions of the Prophet: Volume 1*, 87. Substituted *Allah* for God.

32. Original translation © 2010 by Kenneth S. Cohen, used with permission.

33. Composed by Dr. Edward W. Bastian, who provided the rest of the Buddhist verses for this volume.

BIBLIOGRAPHY

'Arabi, Muhyiddin ibn al-. *101 Diamonds from the Oral Tradition of the Glorious Messenger Muhammad*. Ed. and Trans. Lex Hixon/Nur al- Jerrahi and Fariha Fatima al-Jerrahi. New York: Pir Press, 2002.

Black Elk, Wallace, and William S. Lyon. *Black Elk: The Sacred Ways of a Lakota*. San Francisco: Harper San Francisco, 1991.

Chishti, Moinuddin. *The Book of Sufi Healing*. Rochester, Vermont: Inner Traditions, 1991.

DeMallie, Raymond J. ed., *The Sixth Grandfather: Black Elk's Teachings Given to John G. Neihardt*, Lincoln, Nebraska: University of Nebraska Press, 1984.

Helminski, Kabir. *The Knowing Heart: A Sufi Path of Transformation*. Boston: Shambhala Publications, 1999.

Hujwiri, 'Ali B. Thman al-Jullabi al-. *Kashf al-Mahjub of Al Hujwiri: The Oldest Persian Treatise on Sufism*. Trans. Reynold A. Nicholson. London: Luzac and Co., 1976.

Jahanabadi, Shah Kalim Allah. *Kashkul-i Kalimi*. Delhi: Matba'-i Mujtaba'i, n.d..

James, William. *The Principles of Psychology*. New York: Dover Publications, 1950.

Kaplan, Aryeh. *Meditation and the Bible*. York Beach, Maine: Samuel Weiser, 1989.

Keating, Thomas. *Manifesting God*. New York: Lantern Books, 2005.

Khan, Inayat. *Sufi Teachings*. Delhi: Motilal Banarsidass Publishers, 2003.

—. *The Unity of Religious Ideals*. London: The Sufi Movement, 1921.

Kirmani, Amir Khwurd. *Siyar al-awlia'*. Delhi: Matba'-i Muhibb-i Hind, 1885.

Lao Tsu. *Tao Te Ching*. Trans. Gia-Fu Feng and Jane English. New York: Vintage Books, 1989.

Nurbakhsh, Javad. *Traditions of the Prophet: Volume 1*. New York: Khaniqahi-Nimatullahi Publications, 1981.

Nyanaponika Thera. *The Heart of Buddhist Meditation*. New York:

Samuel Weiser, 1973.

Panikkar, Raimundo et al, ed. and trans.. *The Vedic Experience – Mantramanjari: An Anthology of the Vedas for Modern Man and Contemporary Celebration.* Berkeley: University of California Press, 1977.

Rumi, Jalal al-Din. *Masnavi-yi ma'navi.* Ed. Reynold A. Nicholson. Tehran: Intisharat-i Bihnud, 1953/4.

Shantideva. *The Way of the Bodhisattva.* Trans. Padmakara Translation Group. Boston: Shambhala Publications, 1997.

Shikuh, Muhammad Dara. *Majma'-ul-bahrain.* Ed. and Trans. M. Mahfuz-ul-Haq. Calcutta: The Asiatic Society, 1982.

Yatiswarananda, Swami. *Meditation and Spiritual Life.* Kolkata: Advaita Ashrama, 2007.

MISSION OF THE
SPIRITUAL PATHS INSTITUTE

THE SPIRITUAL PATHS INSTITUTE provides educational programs and meditative training by authentic teachers of the world's contemplative traditions. In partnership with each other, our teachers engage students in the spiritual principles, transformative theories, scientific studies, and meditative experiences of such spiritual traditions as Buddhism, Christianity, Hinduism, Islam Sufism, Judaism, Native American, and Taoism.

This uniquely inclusive education and training helps students to develop a mature, comprehensive, and sustainable meditative practice, giving rise to compassion, wisdom, equanimity, meaning, and purpose. The exceptional value of the Spiritual Paths Institute comes from its authentic training in a primary practice along with systematic exposure to a variety of other contemplative traditions. This integrated study profoundly nourishes and strengthens each student's personal practice. The result of this training is a universal InterSpiritual Wisdom that guides us in our personal lives, relationships, professions, and service in the world.

For information about Spiritual Paths programs, go to www.spiritualpaths.net, call: 805-695-0104 or e-mail ed@ spiritualpaths.net.

PIR NETANEL (MU'IN AD-DIN) MILES-YÉPEZ, D.D., is the current head of the Inayati-Maimuni lineage of Sufism, co-founded with Zalman Schachter-Shalomi, fusing the Sufi and Hasidic principles of spirituality and practice espoused by Rabbi Avraham Maimuni in 13th-century Egypt with the teachings of the Ba'al Shem Tov and Hazrat Inayat Khan. He studied History of Religions at Michigan State University and Contemplative Religion at the Naropa Institute before pursuing traditional studies in both Sufism and Hasidism with Zalman Schachter-Shalomi and various other teachers, including Pir Puran Bair and Thomas Atum O'Kane. He likewise counts Father Thomas Keating as an important influence. He has been deeply involved in ecumenical dialogue and is considered a leading thinker in the InterSpiritual and New Monasticism movements. He is the co-author of two critically acclaimed commentaries on Hasidic spirituality, *A Heart Afire: Stories and Teachings of the Early Hasidic Masters* (2009) and *A Hidden Light: Stories and Teachings of Early HaBaD and Bratzlav Hasidism* (2011), the editor of *The Common Heart: An Experience of Interreligious Dialogue* (2006) and *Living Fully, Dying Well: Reflecting on Death to Find Your Life's Meaning* (2009). He currently teaches Contemplative Islam and Sufism in the Department of Religious Studies at Naropa University.

18364150R00147

Printed in Great Britain
by Amazon